OneBook.
DAILY-WEEKLY

The Letter of 1 Peter

Ruth Anne Reese

Seedbed

Cover design by Strange Last Name
Page design and layout by PerfecType, Nashville, Tennessee

Reese Ruth Anne.
The Letter of 1 Peter / Ruth Anne Reese. – Frankin, Tennessee : Seedbed Publishing, ©2019.

pages ; cm. + 1 videodisc – (OneBook. Daily-weekly)

ISBN 9781628246179 (paperback)
ISBN 9781628246216 (DVD)
ISBN 9781628246186 (Mobi)
ISBN 9781628246193 (ePub)
ISBN 9781628246209 (uPDF)

1. Bible. Peter, 1st -- Textbooks. 2. Bible. Peter, 1st -- Study and teaching. 3. Bible. Peter, 1st -- Commentaries.   I. Title. II. Series.

BS2795.55.R43 2019   227/.920071   2019935192

SEEDBED PUBLISHING
Franklin, Tennessee
seedbed.com

CONTENTS

Contents

Contents

WELCOME TO ONEBOOK DAILY-WEEKLY

John Wesley, in a letter to one of his leaders, penned the following:

> O begin! Fix some part of every day for private exercises. You may acquire the taste which you have not: what is tedious at first, will afterwards be pleasant. Whether you like it or not, read and pray daily. It is for your life; there is no other way; else you will be a trifler all your days. . . . Do justice to your own soul; give it time and means to grow. Do not starve yourself any longer. Take up your cross and be a Christian altogether.

Rarely are our lives most shaped by our biggest ambitions and highest aspirations. Rather, our lives are most shaped, for better or for worse, by those small things we do every single day.

At Seedbed, our biggest ambition and highest aspiration is to resource the followers of Jesus to become lovers and doers of the Word of God every single day, to become people of One Book.

To that end, we have created the OneBook Daily-Weekly. First, it's important to understand what this is not: warm, fuzzy, sentimental devotions. If you engage the Daily-Weekly for any length of time, you will learn the Word of God. You will grow profoundly in your love for God, and you will become a passionate lover of people.

How Does the Daily-Weekly Work?

Daily. As the name implies, every day invites a short but substantive engagement with the Bible. Five days a week you will read a passage of Scripture followed by a short segment of teaching and closing with questions for refection and self-examination. On the sixth day, you will review and reflect on the previous five days.

Weekly. Each week, on the seventh day, find a way to gather with at least one other person doing the study. Pursue the weekly guidance for gathering.

Share learning, insight, encouragement, and most important, how the Holy Spirit is working in your lives.

That's it. Depending on the length of the study, when the eight or twelve weeks are done, we will be ready with the next study. On an ongoing basis, we will release new editions of the Daily-Weekly. Over time, those who pursue this course of learning will develop a rich library of Bible learning resources for the long haul.

OneBook Daily-Weekly will develop eight- and twelve-week studies that cover the entire Old and New Testaments. Seedbed will publish new studies regularly so that an ongoing supply of group lessons will be available. All titles will remain accessible, which means they can be used in any order that fits your needs or the needs of your group.

If you are looking for a substantive study to learn Scripture through a steadfast method, look no further.

1 Peter 1:1–12

God's New Family and the Gift of Salvation

ONE

God Chooses Resident Aliens

1 Peter 1:1–2 NASB *Peter, an apostle of Jesus Christ, to those who reside as aliens, scattered throughout Pontus, Galatia, Cappadocia, Asia, and Bithynia, who are chosen ²according to the foreknowledge of God the Father, by the sanctifying work of the Spirit, to obey Jesus Christ and be sprinkled with His blood: May grace and peace be yours in the fullest measure.*

Key Observation. The Father, the Holy Spirit, and Jesus Christ work together to choose, sanctify, and cleanse scattered resident aliens.

Understanding the Word. This week we will look at 1 Peter's opening greeting (1:1–2) and the blessing that follows (1:3–12). Peter introduces himself as an apostle, a person sent by Jesus to carry the good news to new groups of people, and he names the recipients of his letter as "aliens." By choosing to follow Jesus, the people Peter addressed became "resident aliens" in their own cultural setting. They no longer fit easily within their cultural setting, and they were scattered across a vast region (an area about the size of Texas) in Asia Minor (present-day Turkey). Despite their status as resident aliens, they are also identified as chosen by God the Father. Across the vast region of Asia Minor there were tiny pinpricks of light where groups of believers gathered together to celebrate the work of Jesus in their lives. But these little pinpricks of light faced opposition from those around them. In these circumstances, Peter reminds them that they are chosen. They are chosen by God the Father. In the first century, fathers were powerful people who ruled over their families. Ideally, they sought the best for their family and encouraged cooperation for the good of the family unit. God the Father is both loving and powerful, and he knew beforehand that he would choose these resident aliens. God's foreknowledge of the resident aliens and their situation is a word of comfort that reminds them that God has not forgotten them. Long ago God chose Israel to be his people and to carry out his mission in the world (Exod. 19:6). Now, God is choosing this group of scattered aliens to be his people in the Word and to live in a manner worthy of their identity as his children.

Each member of the Trinity is involved in the process of choosing. The Father uses foreknowledge to choose. Then, by means of the Spirit, followers of Jesus are set apart from those around them. Being chosen by God and sanctified (set apart, made holy) by the Spirit results in being made ready and willing to obey Jesus, the One who sacrificed his own blood to cleanse those who trust him. The blood of Jesus is sprinkled on his people to cleanse them just as Moses sprinkled blood on God's people to cleanse them when they entered into covenant relationship with God (Exod. 24:8).

Peter has identified himself. Then he encourages his audience with a reminder that although they are scattered resident aliens, God has chosen them. Finally, he prompts them to remember that as people cleansed by Jesus' blood, they have been set apart for obedience to Jesus. He finishes the opening of the letter by wishing that his audience will experience a multiplication of grace and peace in their lives. Have you received the cleansing work of Jesus and the sanctifying work of the Spirit? If so, then may the gifts of grace and peace multiply in your life.

1. Are you eager to obey Jesus? What does obeying Jesus look like in your own life?

2. In what way(s) have you become a resident alien in your culture because you are chosen by God?

T W O

Welcome to the Family

1 Peter 1:3–5 *Praise be to the God and Father of our Lord Jesus Christ! In his great mercy he has given us new birth into a living hope through the resurrection of Jesus Christ from the dead, ⁴and into an inheritance that can never perish, spoil or fade. This inheritance is kept in heaven for you, ⁵who through faith are shielded by God's power until the coming of the salvation that is ready to be revealed in the last time.*

Key Observation. God has given us new life as his children, members of his household, the church.

Understanding the Word. First Peter 1:3–12 is the next major section of the letter and focuses on the identity of God's people. It begins by praising God for who he is. God is the Father of Jesus, and Jesus is "our Lord," one with authority over believers. God acts out of his mercy, the quality of love that extends forgiveness to those who do not deserve it. Out of his *great* mercy, God gives new birth to believers. This takes place through the power of Jesus' resurrection. We are invited to share in a family relationship with God. This family is characterized by living hope. Jesus' resurrection is the basis for the true and certain hope that we will experience God's full salvation. Our new birth and the hope we experience because of it is not a delusion or a fairy tale but is based in Jesus' triumph over the power of death.

As members of God's family, we receive an inheritance. Unlike an earthly inheritance, this inheritance will not fade away, rot, or be destroyed. The inheritance is kept in heaven. In other words, it is in the very presence of God, and that means that the inheritance can be counted on. It is kept in heaven *for you.* As you read 1 Peter, the word "you" will occur more than fifty times. In English we use the word "you" to refer both to groups and to individuals. In Greek, there are singular and plural forms of "you." Each time the Greek word for "you" is used in 1 Peter, it is plural and refers to a group rather than an individual. In the South, the English idiom "y'all" captures the inclusive, group nature of the word "you" in 1 Peter. The inheritance is not for us as individuals but for the whole of God's family, the church.

God gives birth to his people, promises them an inheritance, and then protects his people until the time when they experience God's full salvation. God deploys his power to shield his people so they can attain salvation. God's protection does not mean that the Christian will not suffer. In fact, 1 Peter will have much to say about suffering on account of one's faith! God shields, but the one who has been given new birth must also trust God. The result will be salvation. In 1 Peter, salvation is something that is experienced now as new birth *and* something that is fully received when Jesus reigns in victory at the end-time. Right now, we only have the reign of Jesus as it was inaugurated on the cross when Jesus triumphed over death and sin. His resurrection proclaims his triumph and is the source of our hope. But in time the veil that is over our eyes will be lifted, and we will experience the fullness of salvation in the very presence of God. Have you experienced the new birth (initial salvation)? Are you longing to see God's salvation fully revealed (final salvation) so that the whole world will be transformed by the loving sacrifice of Jesus? This is the invitation of this passage.

1. What qualities and gifts of God do you observe in these verses? Take time to praise and thank God for these things.

2. What does it mean to you to experience new birth and be part of God's family, the church?

THREE

God, the Source of Joy in the Midst of Trials

1 Peter 1:6–7 *In all this you greatly rejoice, though now for a little while you may have had to suffer grief in all kinds of trials. ⁷These have come so that the proven genuineness of your faith—of greater worth than gold, which perishes even though refined by fire—may result in praise, glory and honor when Jesus Christ is revealed.*

Key Observation. Even though we may suffer for our faith, we can rejoice in our identity as part of the family of God.

Understanding the Word. "In all of this" points us back to yesterday's reading. All that God is and all that God gave us through his great mercy is a source of joy for us. This includes our new birth and its results—living hope, an inheritance, God's protective care for his children, and the anticipation of full salvation in the last time. Our new identity as God's children and as members of God's family is focused on God himself and on what God has done for us.

However, those who are members of God's family may experience suffering *on account of* their faith in Jesus. Peter speaks of "all kind of trials." He is referring to a variety of types of suffering that can happen when people are true to their faith in the midst of a culture that is hostile to Christianity. In the first century this probably included verbal attacks, loss of jobs and resources, accusations and trials because of one's allegiance to Jesus, imprisonment, and on rarer occasions, martyrdom. The church around the world continues to experience suffering because of faithful living in response to Jesus. And as in the first century, this suffering can include the same spectrum of trials that were behind the letter Peter wrote to God's children.

The result of trials that are faithfully endured by Christians is a proven faith. The image that Peter uses is that of a refining fire that is used to purify metals such as gold. When the gold is refined and all the impurities are burned up, what is left behind is proven to be genuine gold. Similarly, those who have been through trials *on account of* their faith and have faithfully endured have genuine faith that has been proven. Such trials cause grief, but they are temporary. What lasts forever is faith and its results.

Yesterday, we saw how salvation begins with new birth; then the life that is received comes to its fullness at the revelation of Jesus in the last time. Today, we see that those who live life faithfully in the midst of suffering on account of their faith receive praise, honor, and glory when Jesus is fully revealed. We rightly regard praise, honor, and glory as things directed to God, but the amazing news is that those who live faithfully when confronted with trials get to share in God's glory. In Western culture, we may not think that we face persecution because of our faith, but the challenge is to live faithfully in whatever circumstances we face.

1. Read back through 1 Peter 1:3–5. What kinds of challenges might you face that would tempt you to turn away from being faithful to God?

2. Can you think of ways that you might be tempted to compromise your faith in Jesus to keep a job, look better in someone else's eyes, not make a scene, or for some other reason?

FOUR

Loving Jesus, Receiving Salvation

1 Peter 1:8–9 *Though you have not seen him, you love him; and even though you do not see him now, you believe in him and are filled with an inexpressible and glorious joy, ⁹for you are receiving the end result of your faith, the salvation of your souls.*

Key Observation. Even though we have not seen Jesus, we grow to love and trust him.

Understanding the Word. Have you ever been so happy you couldn't speak? That is the kind of joy that fills those who come to deeply love Jesus. The people to whom Peter wrote lived in Asia Minor (modern-day Turkey). They had not walked with Jesus in Galilee or seen him crucified outside of Jerusalem or eaten with Jesus after the resurrection. But though they had not seen Jesus in his physical body, they loved Jesus deeply.

First Peter 1:1–7 shows us that Jesus sacrificed himself so his people could be clean and enter into relationship with God (v. 2). Jesus, as God's Son, had an intimate relationship with God the Father (v. 3). Similarly, Christians are children of God who experience new life as a gift from God. Jesus was raised from death in the resurrection. Jesus' triumph over death was the source of their living hope. Jesus was alive and present with God the Father. Christians anticipate that the life they began as God's children continues into eternity. They, like Jesus, are children of God and will continue to experience life in the presence of God even after they taste death. Salvation begins with new birth and extends to that time when Jesus will be fully revealed and will make everything new and set everything right. This was the Jesus that the audience of 1 Peter had not seen but had come to love.

The Christians whom Peter addressed had not seen Jesus when he was on earth, and they did not see him now in a physical form. But they believed in him. In the Bible, "belief" does not mean intellectual assent. It does not mean that they agreed to a certain set of propositions about who Jesus was. Rather, "belief" refers to trust. These Christians loved Jesus and understood that he was trustworthy and reliable. When we know that someone is completely worthy of our trust and will never let us down, it makes us deeply happy and full of joy.

The result of these early believers' trust was that they were obtaining salvation. Peter saw salvation as a process. It was not a one-time commitment to God or Jesus that happened in the past. Instead, salvation was an ongoing outcome of their continued lives of faithfulness. In Greek, the word "soul" can refer to one's life, so the salvation they were experiencing was something that was taking place in their lives *now*. They would not have to wait until they died to receive salvation; rather, salvation was animating their lives right now, and it would continue to do so as they walked in faithful, day-to-day relationship with their Father, who had chosen them and given them new birth.

Like these Christians, we have not seen Jesus either, but I hope you have come to love and trust him. I hope you have experienced the joy that comes from knowing Jesus. You can always ask to love and trust Jesus more fully and seek to experience the joy that comes from knowing him.

1. If salvation is a process, how are you experiencing salvation right now?

2. What does it mean to have your life animated by salvation?

3. How does Peter's understanding of salvation compare and contrast with what you have understood about salvation?

FIVE

The Great Gift of Salvation

1 Peter 1:10–12 *Concerning this salvation, the prophets, who spoke of the grace that was to come to you, searched intently and with the greatest care, [11]trying to find out the time and circumstances to which the Spirit of Christ in them was pointing when he predicted the sufferings of the Messiah and the glories that would follow. [12]It was revealed to them that they were not serving themselves but* *you, when they spoke of the things that have now been told you by those who have preached the gospel to you by the Holy Spirit sent from heaven. Even angels long to look into these things.*

Key Observation. Salvation is a gift of God's grace that the prophets searched for and that angels want to look into.

Understanding the Word. Prophets are called by God to speak on his behalf. Prophets were part of Israel from its very earliest days. Moses was a prophet (Deut. 18:18) who spoke to Israel and communicated to them the message of God's deliverance and covenant. Subsequent prophets, such as Samuel, Elijah, Isaiah, Jeremiah, and many others, also spoke God's message to his people. But Peter tells us that what the prophets were really searching for was the salvation that Christians experience when they enter into the new life that God made possible through Jesus. This salvation is identified as "the grace that was to come to you." Grace is a gift. It is not something earned or deserved but rather freely given. The prophets searched diligently to find out when that gift would arrive and what circumstances would bring it about. In fact, Peter says that it was the Spirit of Christ that was nudging them toward the predictions of what would unfold at this time of salvation.

The prophets predicted that the Messiah would suffer and that glorious things would follow that suffering. One example of this is from Isaiah 53, a passage that Peter will quote in chapter 2. There the Lord's servant is depicted as "a man of sorrows and acquainted with grief" (v. 3 NASB). Later in the passage he is pierced, crushed, oppressed, and afflicted. But the result of all of this suffering is that "he bore the sin of many, and made intercession for the transgressors" (v. 12). Sin is a weight that is now carried by Jesus so that we don't have to carry it. And the glories (plural) that follow are all the people who experience the weight of sin lifted from their lives and who find new lives filled with rejoicing. When the prophets wrote of such things—both suffering and glories—they were not doing this for themselves. It was for all those who would have the chance to hear the good news of Jesus' death on their behalf and would come to share in both the suffering and the glory of Jesus.

The people to whom Peter was writing had heard the good news about Jesus through messengers who explained what God had done for them through the life, death, and resurrection of Jesus. This message was enabled by the power of the Holy Spirit at work in those who proclaimed the good news. The message they received was the same message that the prophets had proclaimed before Jesus was ever born: that God's gift would be to send a Messiah, a servant-king, who would remove the burden of sin and bring new life to his people and his kingdom. Even the angels wanted to see the transformation of lives through God's gift to the world—Jesus.

1. In many ways, 1 Peter 1:3–12 is all about salvation. Take a moment to reflect on your own experience of salvation. How did you come to experience new birth?

2. Are you ready to share the message of God's gift of salvation with others? How might you grow in this area?

WEEK ONE

GATHERING DISCUSSION OUTLINE

A. **Open session in prayer.** Ask that God would astonish us anew with fresh insight from God's Word and transform us into the disciples that Jesus desires us to become.

B. **Read 1 Peter 1:1–12 out loud.** You might consider having each member of the group read a verse or asking several people to each read three or four verses.

C. **View video for this week's readings.**

D. What were key insights or takeaways that you gained from your reading during the week and from watching the video commentary? In particular, how did these help you to grow in your faith and understanding of Scripture this week? What parts of the Bible lesson or study raised questions for you?

E. **One main point from this week is:** *God's plan has always been for us to find security in him and in his people by inviting us into a new set of family relationships.*

F. **Discuss questions selected from the daily readings.**

1. **KEY OBSERVATION:** The Father, the Holy Spirit, and Jesus Christ work together to choose, sanctify, and cleanse scattered resident aliens.

   DISCUSSION QUESTION: In what way(s) have you become a resident alien in your culture because you are chosen by God?

2. **KEY OBSERVATION:** God has given us new life as his children, members of his household, the church.

   DISCUSSION QUESTION: What does it mean to you to experience new birth and be part of God's family, the church?

3. **KEY OBSERVATION:** Even though we may suffer for our faith, we can rejoice in our identity as part of the family of God.

   DISCUSSION QUESTION: Read back through 1 Peter 1:3–5. What kinds of challenges might you face that would tempt you to turn away from being faithful to God?

4. **KEY OBSERVATION:** Even though we have not seen Jesus, we grow to love and trust him.

   DISCUSSION QUESTION: If salvation is a process, how are you experiencing salvation right now?

5. **KEY OBSERVATION:** Salvation is a gift of God's grace that the prophets searched for and that angels want to look into.

   DISCUSSION QUESTION: Are you ready to share the message of God's gift of salvation with others? How might you grow in this area?

G. **As the study concludes, consider specific ways that this week's Bible lesson invites you to grow and calls you to change.** How do this week's scriptures call us to think differently? How do they challenge us to change in order to align ourselves with God's work in the world? What specific actions can we take to apply the insights of the lesson to our daily lives? What kind of person does our Bible lesson call each of us to become?

H. **Close session with prayer.** Emphasize God's ongoing work of transformation in our lives in preparation for loving mission and service in the world. Pray for missing class members as well as for people whom we need to invite to join our study.

WEEK TWO

1 Peter 1:13–25

We Are Called to Be Holy as God Is Holy

ONE

Set Your Hope

1 Peter 1:13 ESV *Therefore, preparing your minds for action, and being sober-minded, set your hope fully on the grace that will be brought to you at the revelation of Jesus Christ.*

Key Observation. Hope is a defining characteristic of those who belong to the family of God.

Understanding the Word. In our study this week of 1 Peter 1:13–25, Peter turns from the introduction of God and God's work of forming a new family to a description of how that family should live (vv. 3–12). He knows that those to whom he is writing face a variety of trials on account of their faith, and he wants to encourage them to live well even when they face challenging circumstances (vv. 6–7). His desire is that they will look like their Father and will exhibit hope, trust, and love in their lives (1:14–16).

The main instruction in 1 Peter 1:13 is "set your hope." Like all the other instructions in 1 Peter, this directive is addressed to the whole group. All of you together set your hope on grace. Hope takes place in the context of the family of God, to whom God has given life. The hope that the believers have is based on grace. We have already seen that grace is God's gift of salvation—both in the new birth they received from the Father and in the full salvation they will receive when Jesus sets everything right in this world. This gift of salvation creates a new life—a life distinct from those who do not belong to

Jesus. It is a life that is set apart and filled with love that results in obedience. In other words, we don't obey God to earn salvation or to earn God's attention. We obey God because we know that we are God's beloved, chosen children and that comes to impact our whole life.

Philo was a Jewish philosopher who lived around the same time as Peter. He described hope as "the fountain of all men's lives" and "the source of all happiness."[1] Hope is the emotion that enables us to set a goal and pursue it. In the Old Testament, the most common object of hope is God. As just one example, in Psalm 42:5–6 the psalmist wrote, "Hope in God; for I shall again praise him, my salvation, and my God" (ESV). It is not surprising that the hope that Christians have is based on the grace of God and anticipates the return of Jesus to this world.

There are two characteristics that accompany Christian hope. The first one is having a mind that is prepared for action. In the original Greek, this is a very vivid metaphor that could be translated into English as something like "roll up the sleeves of your mind." In other words, be alert and ready to go. At the same time, Christians are to be sober. This is a state of calm and self-restraint. Peter encourages Christians who are intent on setting their hope on the gift of God's grace to be ready and watchful, steady and calm. Because they know that their hope is in the most trustworthy and reliable person, there is no need for anxiety, agitation, or fear.

1. What does setting your hope look like in your life?

2. How does gathering with other Christians help you set your hope on the gift of salvation that you have received?

3. What keeps you from hoping fully?

---

1. Philo, *On Rewards and Punishments*, 2.11.

TWO

Be Holy

1 Peter 1:14–16 ESV *As obedient children, do not be conformed to the passions of your former ignorance, ¹⁵but as he who called you is holy, you also be holy in all your conduct, ¹⁶since it is written, "You shall be holy, for I am holy."*

Key Observation. It is a great privilege to be invited to share in the holiness of our Father.

Understanding the Word. Have you ever met a family in which the children looked so much like their parents that there was no question who the parents were? Or perhaps, the sayings "Like father, like son" or "Like mother, like daughter" ring true for you. Both of these demonstrate how we recognize the features of parents on their children. In today's verses, we get a picture of how God's children resemble their Father.

Peter reminds his audience of their identity as "obedient children" (vv. 2, 14). They were not always God's children. At one time they had lived in ignorance. They did not know that God knew them (v. 2) or that he would give them new birth (v. 3) and a permanent inheritance (v. 4). Neither did they know they would experience the healing and deliverance of salvation. Instead, they did whatever they felt like doing—even the things that were contrary to the desires of God's heart. But now that they are God's children, they are not to allow themselves to be molded by their previous, ungodly passions.

Are you being molded by ungodly longings? If so, I invite you to turn your attention to the character of your Father, the holy God. God is calling you. Ask God to help you look like him. It is also good to seek the counsel of other godly Christians. Again, the instruction is to all of us together. We are to work together so that we are not conformed to those former ungodly desires. You are not in the struggle alone.

God invites us as his children to be holy. Sometimes we are tempted to think that holiness is beyond our reach. Or, even worse, we think that holiness is all about looking virtuous. But in reality, God invites us to look like our Father, the Holy One. To be holy is to be set apart. God is completely set apart from his creation in a way that makes him majestic and worthy of awe. We cannot imitate this. But God is also holy in an ethical sense. His holy actions are just and loving. We, too, can be people of justice and love. In Leviticus 19:2, God instructed the people of Israel to be holy as he was holy. The next several chapters in Leviticus are practical instructions showing Israel how to live in just and loving ways with their families, neighbors, and strangers. Peter is instructing the new family of God to be holy in all their conduct. In other words, they are to display love and justice toward others because this is what holiness looks like in practice. When we see the church treating others with love and advocating for justice, we are seeing God's holy character on display. When we walk in the love and justice that flows out of our Father's holiness, we are exhibiting the same character our Father exhibits.

1. What would help you not be molded by ungodly desires, and what would help you pursue God's holy character?

2. What are some practical ways that you can practice holiness (loving and just actions toward others) in your day-to-day life at home, at work, and in other places you go?

THREE

Conduct Yourselves with Awe

1 Peter 1:17–19 ESV *And if you call on him as Father who judges impartially according to each one's deeds, conduct yourselves with fear throughout the time of your exile, ¹⁸knowing that you were ransomed from the futile ways inherited from your forefathers, not with perishable things such as silver or gold, ¹⁹but with the precious blood of Christ, like that of a lamb without blemish or spot.*

Key Observation. God paid a high price to redeem us, and he asks that we live our daily lives in awe of him.

Understanding the Word. Take a moment to think about the difference between a father and an impartial judge. The father loves, defends, and cares for his children. The judge seeks justice based on the actions of each person. The judge does not base his decision on the relationship he has with the defendant. Peter reminds his readers that even though they are God's children, they cannot get away with doing whatever they please. They cannot use their position as God's children to escape his judgment. God is their Father, and they can call on him. But the instruction in verse 17 is to conduct yourselves with fear. The word "fear" can be translated as "awe" or "reverence." In their daily lives, Christians are to be mindful of God's awesome holiness and his call on their lives to be holy like him. In light of this, their whole life is to be lived in the presence of God. Awe and reverence are not reserved for church. This attitude of awe and reverence shapes every bit of the life of Christians who recognize their Father as both loving and just. It is hard to live a holy life (a life of integrity and love) in a culture that laughs at holiness. But this is the life that Christians are called to. It is possible that when you practice living a life of love and integrity that on some days you will feel like an illegal immigrant or a resident alien in your own cultural context. You may find that you no longer fit in or belong because you are not doing the things that everyone around you is doing.

There are two contrasts in verses 18–19. First, there is a contrast between good conduct (v. 17) and futile ways of living (v. 18). Second, there is a contrast between perishable things, like silver and gold (v. 18), and the precious blood of Jesus (v. 19). As Christians, they have been ransomed or redeemed. This language describes purchasing people from slavery. In the Old Testament, God ransomed the people of Israel from Egypt (Deut. 7:8). He delivered them from slavery. When God redeemed Israel, they became his. In the same way, when God redeems Christians with the precious blood of his Son Jesus, they become his. As their Father and as their redeemer, he expects good conduct.

This expectation is heightened because of the cost. He did not buy them with gold and silver. Instead, he purchased them with the blood of Jesus. Jesus' blood is compared with the blood of a spotless, unblemished lamb. In the Old Testament, the blood of the perfect lamb is spread across the doorposts at Passover. This protects the people from death. In the religious rituals of Israel, the perfect lamb is the sacrifice offered for sin. Now, the blood of God's Son, Jesus, becomes the perfect sacrifice that delivers his children from sin and death.

1. How does seeing God as both Father and Judge help you think about God's character and actions? How does it help you think about your relationship with God?

2. What are some practical examples of how you live out the instruction to have good conduct in your daily life?

FOUR

Your Faith and Hope Are in God

1 Peter 1:20–21 ESV *He [Christ] was foreknown before the foundation of the world but was made manifest in the last times for the sake of you [21] who through him are believers in God, who raised him from the dead and gave him glory, so that your faith and hope are in God.*

Key Observation. You have become believers through Christ.

Understanding the Word. Throughout Scripture, God is affirmed as the Creator of the world. Here, Peter uses the imagery of a building to describe creation. But the real focus is not on creation but on what God knew before space and time began. God already knew Christ long before he created the world. In verses 1–2, Peter showed us the Father, Son, and Holy Spirit working together to select, purify, and cleanse the chosen people of God. Now Peter reminds us that God knew Christ before the world began. The intimate relationship between God and Christ is implied here.

But even though God knew Christ, the world did not know him. Instead, Jesus Christ was not revealed until the "last times." The last times begin with Jesus' arrival in the world and continue until the day when Jesus Christ will return. This means that we, like the early church, are living in the last times. Like the early church, we have the privilege of living after the life, death, and resurrection of Jesus. These events made it possible for us to experience deliverance from sin and an ability to grow into lives that look like the life of our holy Father. In other words, we live faithfully now while also anticipating that final day when Jesus Christ will return.

The title "Christ" means "the anointed one." It is the Greek word that translates the Old Testament word *Messiah*. God knew that there would be a chosen one who would redeem (v. 19) and deliver his people from their futile ways of living (v. 18). Indeed, when Jesus was revealed, it was for your sake. Remember that "you" is plural, so this means that it is for the sake of the whole church, those who believe. God knew Christ in advance and was willing to pay a great price to save his people.

Peter is clear that our ability to believe in God comes about through Christ ("through him"). Again, remember that believing is about both what we accept with our minds and how we live our daily lives. We might describe it as believing faithfulness toward God. And it is God who raised Jesus from the dead. The New Testament makes it very clear that after his death Jesus was suddenly filled with breath and revived. Instead, throughout the New Testament, God is the agent who raises Jesus from death. God's raising of Jesus from death has been described as a vindication of Jesus' faithful life and death in relationship with the Father God. In addition, God gives Jesus glory. Glory is the expression of God's presence. It is sometimes described as a great weight or as a light. Here God extends glory to Jesus. The result of God's action is that the faith and hope of believers is strengthened. What God can do for Jesus, believers can trust God will do for them. They too will come to experience resurrection, and they too will share in God's glory.

1. Take a few minutes to list out the privileges you have as one who lives in the last times. What do you know and have access to that was not available to those who lived before Jesus?

FIVE

Love One Another Earnestly

1 Peter 1:22–25 ESV *Having purified your souls by your obedience to the truth for a sincere brotherly love, love one another earnestly from a pure heart, ²³since you have been born again, not of perishable seed but of imperishable, through the living and abiding word of God; ²⁴for "All flesh is like grass and all its glory like the flower of grass. The grass withers, and the flower falls, ²⁵but the word of the Lord remains forever." And this word is the good news that was preached to you.*

Key Observation. Our love for one another flows out of the new life we have received from God.

Understanding the Word. First Peter continues with family language that is rooted in our new birth. The instruction in this portion of the text is to love each other deeply. Before Peter gives this instruction, he reminds his audience that they have already purified themselves by their obedience to the truth. Verses 22–23 communicate two truths about the good news. First, we cannot make ourselves pure. Verse 3 says we receive the gift of new birth. We do not earn this purity that comes from God. Second, we are asked to grow up as God's children and do our part. We are given the gift of being able to participate in the process of becoming pure. When we put these two things together, we see that God gives us holiness *and* enables us to participate in becoming holy. One of the ways we participate is by our obedience to the truth. Here, the truth refers to the good news that Jesus cleansed us from sin and entered into covenant relationship with us. Obedience is a form of submission. When we obey, we are saying, "Lord, who you are and the message you proclaim are right and good. I submit myself to you and your ways. I will follow you." These are words of obedience. As we obey, we become purer, and we gain the ability to love those around us more fully and continuously.

We are to love each other from a pure heart because of God's gift of new life. The new life we receive comes about through the imperishable Word of God. Peter quotes from Isaiah 40:6–8. Isaiah 40 is about God's comfort of Israel when they were living in exile and his promise to lead them out of exile and back to the promised land. Even though things such as grass and flowers wither and die, God's promise (his word) is forever. Peter's audience is also experiencing a life of exile. They are described as resident aliens (v. 1). The reminder that God's word is forever can comfort them too. The word that is forever is the same good news that was preached to them. This is the message of Jesus, his life, death, and resurrection. Even though their circumstances are fragile, they can be certain that God's message in Jesus is secure.

God has given us new birth by means of his imperishable word. This is the reason we are able to love each other. We are invited to participate in becoming more like God by being made pure through our obedience (vv. 14–16). At the same time, there are some people within our church family that can be difficult to love. How might we go about obeying Jesus and his good news message even when someone is difficult to love? Remember, we are God's beloved children, secure in his eternal Word.

1. How might you come to experience God's holiness and love more fully?

2. Describe in some detail a time when you received love from another member of your church family. What impact did that have on you and why?

WEEK TWO

GATHERING DISCUSSION OUTLINE

A. **Open session in prayer.** Ask that God would astonish us anew with fresh insight from God's Word and transform us into the disciples that Jesus desires us to become.

B. **Read 1 Peter 1:13–25 out loud.** You might consider having each member of the group read a verse or asking several people to each read three or four verses.

C. **View video for this week's readings.**

D. What were key insights or takeaways that you gained from your reading during the week and from watching the video commentary? In particular, how did these help you to grow in your faith and understanding of Scripture this week? What parts of the Bible lesson or study raised questions for you?

E. **One main point from this week is**: *As redeemed believers in Jesus Christ, we are called to be holy as God the Father is holy.*

F. **Discuss questions selected from the daily readings.**

1. **KEY OBSERVATION:** Hope is a defining characteristic of those who belong to the family of God.

    DISCUSSION QUESTION: How does gathering with other Christians help you set your hope on the gift of salvation that you have received?

2. **KEY OBSERVATION:** It is a great privilege to be invited to share in the holiness of our Father.

   DISCUSSION QUESTION: What would help you not be molded by ungodly desires, and what would help you pursue God's holy character?

3. **KEY OBSERVATION:** God paid a high price to redeem us, and he asks that we live our daily lives in awe of him.

   DISCUSSION QUESTION: What are some practical examples of how you live out the instruction to have good conduct in your daily life?

4. **KEY OBSERVATION:** You have become believers through Christ.

   DISCUSSION QUESTION: Take a few minutes to list out the privileges you have as one who lives in the last times. What do you know and have access to that was not available to those who lived before Jesus?

5. **KEY OBSERVATION:** Our love for one another flows out of the new life we have received from God.

   DISCUSSION QUESTION: How might you come to experience God's holiness and love more fully?

G. **As the study concludes, consider specific ways that this week's Bible lesson invites you to grow and calls you to change.** How do this week's scriptures call us to think differently? How do they challenge us to change in order to align ourselves with God's work in the world? What specific actions should we take to apply the insights of the lesson to our daily lives? What kind of person does our Bible lesson call each of us to become?

H. **Close session with prayer.** Emphasize God's ongoing work of transformation in our lives in preparation for loving mission and service in the world. Pray for missing class members as well as for people whom we need to invite to join our study.

1 Peter 2:1–10

Long to Be Made into God's Dwelling Place

ONE

Crave

1 Peter 2:1–3 *Therefore, rid yourselves of all malice and all deceit, hypocrisy, envy, and slander of every kind. ²Like newborn babies, crave pure spiritual milk, so that by it you may grow up in your salvation, ³now that you have tasted that the Lord is good.*

Key Observation. If you want to grow up, then crave the pure milk that comes from God.

Understanding the Word. This week we will complete the second major section of 1 Peter. First, we looked at the introduction (vv. 1–2). Then, we looked at the foundation for our identity as the people of God (vv. 3–12). In our current section (1:13–2:10), we are looking at instructions that flow out of our identity as God's people. This week focuses a little more on our identity as God's family and introduces the idea that we are God's temple.

At the end of last week, we saw that God gives us the gift of new life. In 1 Peter, the whole Trinity is involved in the work of purifying believers. The Spirit sets us apart and makes us holy (1:2), the blood of Jesus cleanses us (1:3, 18), and the Father gives us new birth (1:3). At the same time, we are invited to participate in becoming holy (1:15–16, 22). Out of this gift of new life comes a life of continuous love for fellow believers (1:22–23).

Chapter 2 continues this theme by showing how the church can love one another. We are to put off activities that destroy love. This includes all malice (evil intentions). When we have hearts that are shaped by God's holiness and by love for one another, we do not wish evil toward others. We are not to deceive one another. This includes outright lies as well as misdirection. It also includes other kinds of speech that manipulate others into believing untruths. We should not be hypocrites. We all long for authentic relationships, but we cannot have real relationships with those who are play-acting or pretending. Honesty and integrity are part of loving behavior. We are to put aside envy. This is the desire to have what belongs to others. Envy is not confined to possessions. We might also envy even the spiritual gifts of others. It is important to know that whatever you have—possessions, gifts, or anything else—comes from God and is given to you as God's beloved child. There is no need to look with envy at anyone else.

Rather than envying others, God wants us to crave his milk. This milk is pure. It hasn't been watered down. Instead, it is exactly what you need to live the spiritual life that you have been called to. Longing for and drinking deeply from the milk of God produces growth. Just as newborn babies are desperate to drink their mother's milk, we should have the same deep longing for the things of God. When babies drink milk, they grow and mature. The same thing happens to us when we drink the spiritual nourishment that God gives. We grow into salvation. In 1 Peter, salvation is a process that begins at conversion and is completed when Jesus returns. During our lifetime, we are growing in our experience of God's deliverance, healing, and new life. We can describe this experience as tasting that the Lord is good (Psalm 34:8).

1. Are there things in your life that you need to take off or set aside in order to be able to love those around you?

2. How are you drinking deeply of the life that God has to offer you?

TWO

The Church Is God's Temple

1 Peter 2:4–5 *As you come to him, the living Stone—rejected by humans but chosen by God and precious to him—⁵you also, like living stones, are being built into a spiritual house to be a holy priesthood, offering spiritual sacrifices acceptable to God through Jesus Christ.*

Key Observation. God makes us like Jesus and then uses us to build his temple.

Understanding the Word. Today and tomorrow, we are going to be looking at 1 Peter 2:4–8. These verses are sometimes referred to as the "stone passages" because images of stones appear in both verses. This imagery is connected to our earlier metaphor of family. We are becoming God's house. And it is connected to a new image as well—a temple. The word "house" can also mean temple.

Our passage begins "as you come to him." In the previous verses we read about longing like babies for pure spiritual milk and tasting that God is good. Our longing should draw us toward Jesus, and we take steps to move closer to him. Jesus is the living Stone. Stones, of course, do not live, so this is a metaphor. It reminds us that Jesus is resurrected and lives and reigns with the Father and the Spirit. This is the living Stone to which we draw near.

Humans rejected Jesus, the living Stone. During his life many people heard Jesus' message but chose not to follow him. And, in the end, they put Jesus to death—the ultimate rejection of his identity as God's chosen Messiah and the ultimate rejection of his message. But in the sight of God, Jesus was chosen and precious. Remember that our audience was also experiencing rejection by those around them who did not believe the message of Jesus. Like Jesus, our audience is also a group of people whom God has chosen (1 Peter 1:1).

In fact, believers, like Jesus, are also living stones. When we experience new birth, we become like Christ. Together, we are being built by God into a spiritual house. We do not build ourselves into God's house. Rather this is something that God does for us. It is also not about any one individual person becoming God's house. In other words, this is not about our individual bodies being God's temple. Instead, we might imagine a building site. God is the builder, and he is creating a house (temple) where he will live. He has created a whole host of living stones through the new birth. Now, he selects those stones and places them together to form the walls of his house. The group together becomes God's dwelling place.

Together they become a holy priesthood. The role of priests is to mediate between God and others. One thing the gathered people of God do is help others enter the presence of God. The other thing that priests do is offer sacrifices. These sacrifices are acts of worship, repentance, and thanksgiving. Today, the people of God continue to gather to acknowledge that together they form the temple God built. God has built the whole worldwide church as his dwelling place. We might think of each local gathering of believers as a room in God's greater temple. And when the church gathers, it offers God sacrifices of praise and repentance.

1. How does thinking about the worldwide church as God's temple impact how you think about your own local church?

2. How do you experience the sacrifices of praise, thanksgiving, and repentance in your communal life with other believers?

3. What stands out to you about the image of being living stones?

THREE

Jesus Is the Cornerstone

1 Peter 2:6–8 *For in Scripture it says: "See, I lay a stone in Zion, a chosen and precious cornerstone, and the one who trusts in him will never be put to shame."*

⁷Now to you who believe, this stone is precious. But to those who do not believe, "The stone the builders rejected has become the cornerstone,"

⁸and, "A stone that causes people to stumble and a rock that makes them fall."

They stumble because they disobey the message—which is also what they were destined for.

Key Observation. We all have a choice to make. We can choose to follow Jesus or to reject Jesus.

Understanding the Word. Our Scripture reading today is woven from three Old Testament passages and comments by Peter. Our Old Testament was the Scripture of the early church. They read it to understand Jesus. And the early church read the Old Testament in light of the life, death, and resurrection of Jesus. In other words, Jesus and the Old Testament interpreted each other. The early church also interpreted the Old Testament differently. For the early church, texts that shared the same word could interpret each other. When these were woven together with comments from a teacher, they were called *midrash.* Today's passage is a midrash where all the passages share the Greek word that we have translated as "stone." Peter adds his own comments to weave these passages together. In 1 Peter 2:4 Jesus is already identified as the living Stone chosen by God. So, all the references to a stone in 1 Peter 2:6–8 are about Jesus.

First Peter 2:6 comes from Isaiah 28:16. Isaiah 28 is about corrupt rulers in Jerusalem who were characterized by death and deceit. In contrast, God promises to build a new city filled with justice and integrity. Peter takes this text from Isaiah to explain that the new thing that God is building begins with Jesus. When the church hears this, they will be reminded that God's foundation will be just and true and full of life.

First Peter 2:7 begins with Peter's interpretive comment. Those who believe find the Stone, Jesus, precious. We honor and treasure the One who is precious to us, Jesus. Those who do not believe find out that what they rejected is actually the cornerstone of all God is doing. This quote comes from Psalm 118:22. Psalm 118 is a song that celebrates God's victory over Israel's enemies. The kings around Israel mocked and rejected Israel's king. But God fought on behalf of his chosen king and made what others rejected into the cornerstone of Israel. In 1 Peter, those who do not believe are compared to builders. When builders create a building, they select a stone to be the foundation of the building. Those who do not believe are like builders who look at a stone and say, "No, that one is not the cornerstone." But, the stone they reject, Jesus, is God's chosen foundation.

This very stone will cause those who do not believe to stumble and fall. This last quotation comes from Isaiah 8:14. Those who refuse Jesus are those who disobey the message about Jesus. Both belief and disbelief are actions. First Peter characterizes belief as obedience and disbelief as disobedience. So, following or rejecting Jesus is not solely about what we affirm with our minds. It is also about what we affirm with our actions.

Peter encourages the church by reminding them that Jesus is the foundation of God's house. God is the builder. Our choice is to honor the one God has chosen or to reject Jesus and continue on our way.

1. What does sharing the good news about Jesus look like as the church?

2. Have you seen disbelief connected to disobedience in your own life? What were the results?

3. Have you moved from disbelief to belief? How did that happen?

FOUR

Chosen with a Purpose

1 Peter 2:9 *But you are a chosen people, a royal priesthood, a holy nation, God's special possession, that you may declare the praises of him who called you out of darkness into his wonderful light.*

Key Observation. It is the privilege of the church to share God's good news with the world.

Understanding the Word. First Peter 2:9 begins with the word "but." This is a word of contrast. Those who believe are God's chosen people, in contrast to those who do not believe, those who disobey, those who stumble against the message of Jesus. This is the end of the first major section of 1 Peter. And it ends with a strong parallel with 1 Peter 1:1. The people who were first addressed as chosen are reminded again that God has selected them.

This verse alludes to Exodus 19:4–6. Exodus begins with God delivering his people from slavery in Egypt. He brought them through the Red Sea. Now, in Exodus 19, he has gathered them at Mount Sinai. There God will make a covenant with his people. A covenant is a promise between two parties. The almighty God promises that he will bind himself to Israel, he will love and protect them, and give them the land of Israel. In return, God asks that Israel bind themselves to him in obedience and faithfulness. In that context, God says to Israel, "You yourselves have seen what I did to the Egyptians, and how I bore you on eagles' wings and brought you to Myself. Now then, if you will indeed obey My voice and keep My covenant, you shall be *My own possession* among all the peoples, for all the earth is Mine; and you shall be to Me *a kingdom of priests and a holy nation*" (NASB, emphasis added). The words in italics are alluded to in 1 Peter 2:9. Peter reminds the church that just as God chose Israel, now God is choosing the church.

The church is God's special possession, and it has two roles to play in the world. First, the church is to be a royal priesthood. A priesthood is a whole group of people who are appointed by God to mediate between God and humanity. They help others come into the presence of God. This particular priesthood is royal and represents the King to the world.

The second role of the church is to be a holy nation. A nation is a group of people with a shared identity. The shared identity of the church is holiness. We remember that the thesis of this book is that the church is in the process of becoming holy like God (1:14–16).

Both of these identities are outward oriented. The church is in the business of telling others about what God has done for them. There was a time when we lived in darkness, but God has brought the church into his light. As representatives of our King and as a new nation that is becoming more and more like our King, we have a purpose. Our purpose is to let the world know what God has done through Jesus Christ. He has redeemed those in slavery. He has washed those who are dirty. He has made holy those who were unclean. This is not our own doing. It is our joy to share.

1. What makes the church more like God and different from the world around it?

2. How has your church been actively engaged in telling the world about God's light?

FIVE

Recipients of Mercy

1 Peter 2:10 *Once you were not a people, but now you are the people of God; once you had not received mercy, but now you have received mercy.*

Key Observation. God, out of his mercy, is creating a new people for himself—the church.

Understanding the Word. Today, we will finish up 2:1–10 and review the message of 1 Peter so far. Peter finishes his word of encouragement in 2:10 with a quotation from Hosea. In Hosea, God calls the prophet Hosea to marry a prostitute. This marriage is a picture of the relationship between God and Israel (Hosea 1:2–3). So, Hosea married Gomer. When Gomer gave birth to her second child, a daughter, the prophet was told to name her "No Mercy" (1:6 ESV). Then Gomer had a third child, a son. And God said the child's name was "Not My People" (1:8–9). Despite God's judgment against unfaithful Israel, God still promised to keep the covenant he had made with his people. He promises that he will restore and protect his people. Justice, steadfast love, and mercy will characterize the life between God and his people. When the people are restored, the land that sustains them with food (grain, wine, and oil) is also restored. This is the context in which God says to Not My People, "You are my people" (2:18–23) and to No Mercy that he will have mercy. Peter uses this story from the Old Testament to remind his readers that they were not God's people but God chose them. While the world around them may think they are strange and do not belong, God chooses them as his family. There was a time before their experience of new birth when they had not experienced the mercy of God. Peter has already reminded them that their experience of new birth flows out of the great mercy of God (1 Peter 1:3). Now, all those who experience the new birth have received the mercy of God.

First Peter repeatedly affirms the identity of the church as God's new household. This begins with new birth initiated by God the Father (1:3). At the very heart of the book where Peter lays out his thesis statement, we are identified as obedient children (1:14). Obedient children are invited to become holy as their Father is holy. Then we are reminded that we are babies, who long to be fed pure, spiritual milk (2:2). Now this family is being built into the place where God dwells—both the household of God and the temple of God. And this family is invited into God's purposes—sharing the message of all that God has done to bring his people out of darkness and into light.

God's family, however, are also resident aliens. They do not look like or act like the world around them. They are living like strangers in their world. This does not mean that this world is not their home, and that they are just waiting to go to heaven. What it means is that their experience is more like the experience of a refugee who finds everything strange and turned upside down. Nothing about their culture is normal anymore. They must find a new normal as God's holy people living in their cities, countries, and neighborhoods.

1. How has God shown mercy to you individually and to the church as a whole?

2. How is God shaping your local community to be part of God's people, God's worldwide family?

WEEK THREE

GATHERING DISCUSSION OUTLINE

A. **Open session in prayer.** Ask that God would astonish us anew with fresh insight from God's Word and transform us into the disciples that Jesus desires us to become.

B. **Read 1 Peter 2:1–10 out loud.** You might consider having each member of the group read a verse or asking several people to each read three or four verses.

C. **View video for this week's readings.**

D. What were key insights or takeaways that you gained from your reading during the week and from watching the video commentary? In particular, how did these help you to grow in your faith and understanding of Scripture this week? What parts of the Bible lesson or study raised questions for you?

E. **One main point from this week is:** *Jesus is the foundation of the church God is building. Those who follow him are like living stones in the church.*

F. **Discuss questions selected from the daily readings.**

1. **KEY OBSERVATION:** If you want to grow up, then crave the pure milk that comes from God.

   DISCUSSION QUESTION: How are you drinking deeply of the life that God has to offer you?

2. **KEY OBSERVATION:** God makes us like Jesus and then uses us to build his temple.

    DISCUSSION QUESTION: How do you experience the sacrifices of praise, thanksgiving, and repentance in your communal life with other believers?

3. **KEY OBSERVATION:** We all have a choice to make. We can choose to follow Jesus or to reject Jesus.

    DISCUSSION QUESTION: How have you moved from disbelief to belief? How did that happen?

4. **KEY OBSERVATION:** It is the privilege of the church to share God's good news with the world.

    DISCUSSION QUESTION: How has your church been actively engaged in telling the world about God's light?

5. **KEY OBSERVATION:** God, out of his mercy, is creating a new people for himself—the church.

    DISCUSSION QUESTION: How is God shaping your local community to be part of God's people, God's worldwide family?

G. **As the study concludes, consider specific ways that this week's Bible lesson invites you to grow and calls you to change.** How do this week's scriptures call us to think differently? How do they challenge us to change in order to align ourselves with God's work in the world? What specific actions should we take to apply the insights of the lesson to our daily lives? What kind of person does our Bible lesson call us to become?

H. **Close session with prayer.** Emphasize God's ongoing work of transformation in our lives in preparation for loving mission and service in the world. Pray for missing class members as well as for people whom we need to invite to join our study.

1 Peter 2:11–25

Life in Society as God's Household: Part I

ONE

Household Instructions

1 Peter 2:11–12 NRSV *Beloved, I urge you as aliens and exiles to abstain from the desires of the flesh that wage war against the soul. ¹²Conduct yourselves honorably among the Gentiles, so that, though they malign you as evildoers, they may see your honorable deeds and glorify God when he comes to judge.*

Key Observation. God's new family is called to good works.

Understanding the Word. First Peter 2:11–25 is the beginning of a household code. In the first century, household codes provided instructions on how various members of the household should treat one another. Peter's household code is going to begin by addressing everyone in the house (2:11–17). Then, it addresses slaves (2:18–25). Next week, we will look at the portions addressed to wives (3:1–6) and husbands (3:7), along with a final section addressed to everyone (3:8–12). Remember: these are instructions for God's household. One of Peter's concerns is to show how God's household is to interact with those around it. So, many of the instructions demonstrate how members of God's household are to deal with unbelievers who are not part of the household. It may be tempting to think that the portions of the text addressed to slaves, wives, or husbands do not apply to us if we don't fit into that category.

However, one possibility is that the behavior of the slaves and the wives is designed to set an example for all Christians to follow.

Peter addresses his audience as "Beloved." These are God's children, and he loves them. They are living in their cities as holy exiles (1 Peter 1:1). This distinctive identity sets them apart from those around them. Their identity as God's family is to be lived out. On the one hand, they must abstain from those desires that would destroy them. Instead of being controlled by unholy desires, they are to act with honor and integrity. When practicing abstention, it is best to replace the thing desired with something that is wholesome. In this case, replace ungodly desire with right actions toward the Gentiles, those who are not Christians.

Peter's audience is experiencing a problem. Those who are not Christians see them as evildoers. As Christians, Peter's audience do not participate in the activities of the city that were not in keeping with their call to holiness. They do not go to the temple to worship the emperor or engage in games and other entertainments where people indulge in drunkenness. These choices lead unbelievers to see them as evildoers—as people having the potential to bring down the wrath of the gods for upending the civil order of their community. The response of the Christian community is to continue doing good deeds. The result is that when the judgment day comes, unbelievers will see the good deeds of the Christian community and glorify God. Peter encourages his audience to persevere in good works. They are to act with honor and integrity in their business dealings, in their community work, and in their life at work. Good works includes activities of generosity and provision for others as well. All of these are to characterize the Christian community even when they face rejection or persecution because of their identity as followers of Jesus. Doing good works is a joyful response of love and is part of how the church communicates its identity to the outside world.

1. Are you doing good works as a member of God's family that others can identify? What will help you persevere in doing good works?

2. Have you had an experience where you did the right thing (or a good deed), but it was misunderstood or even seen as evil by those around you?

TWO

Honor Everyone

1 Peter 2:13–17 ESV *Be subject for the Lord's sake to every human institution, whether it be to the emperor as supreme, ¹⁴or to governors as sent by him to punish those who do evil and to praise those who do good. ¹⁵For this is the will of God, that by doing good you should put to silence the ignorance of foolish people. ¹⁶Live as people who are free, not using your freedom as a cover-up for evil, but living as servants of God. ¹⁷Honor everyone. Love the brotherhood. Fear God. Honor the emperor.*

Key Observation. As God's servants, we should honor everyone.

Understanding the Word. Everyone in the first century understood that the household was the fundamental building block of society. The ancient household consisted of mother, father, children, slaves, former slaves, and others. The emperor himself was referred to as the father of the country. Two important values shaped life: honor and kinship. To be an honorable person and act in honorable ways was one of life's highest goals. It was more important than being wealthy. And, it was often connected to one's family. Those who came from high-status families, such as the imperial family, had honor simply because of their birth. Those who had no right to citizenship in the empire were shamed and despised because of their low status. Peter has spent the first part of the book showing the believers that they now belong to the most honorable family—the family of God.

Even as members of God's family, Peter still instructs them to respect the authority of human institutions. Note, these institutions are human and not divine. They are to respect the emperor and his rulers for the Lord's sake. This is a way of honoring God. Their respect for authority cannot be unquestioning. For example, they could not worship Caesar as a god even if it was demanded. Nor could they denounce Jesus before the authorities. But they were asked to yield to the authority of the empire.

First Peter was written at the height of the Roman Empire. The empire used military force to create peace throughout the Mediterranean world. The Romans expected the provinces they ruled to submit to them and honor them.

When Peter instructs his audience of resident aliens to respect the authority of the state, he encourages them to act like the world around them. But they don't act this way because the Romans think they should, but rather for the Lord's sake. They want to act in ways that will not bring shame to the name of Jesus or to God's household. Most of us live in a democracy and must seek wisdom to understand how Peter's words apply to our context. One measure is to ask whether our activities are good, honorable, and bring glory to God and God's household. Another measure is to ask whether the church is truly living as slaves who do the bidding of their Master, God.

Believers are to conduct themselves with honor (2:12) and do good works. This way of life was designed to silence ignorant people—another description of those who do not know Jesus. No matter what their status in life, they were to live as people who were free. But they are not to use their freedom to do evil. They are not to use their status as members of God's family as an excuse for evil. Indeed, they are to see themselves as God's slaves—part of the ancient household.

Finally, Peter instructs them to honor everyone, including the emperor. The emperor is not more important than others. At the center is the command to love their fellow Christians (see 1:22–23) and to fear God (see 1:17).

1. How are you living as a free person who is also a slave of God?

2. Pick one or two of the last four commands (honor the emperor, love the brotherhood, fear God, honor everyone). How do we live that instruction in our world today?

THREE

Unjust Suffering

1 Peter 2:18–20 *Slaves, in reverent fear of God submit yourselves to your masters, not only to those who are good and considerate, but also to those who are harsh. ¹⁹For it is commendable if someone bears up under the pain of unjust suffering because they are conscious of God. ²⁰But how is it to your credit if you receive a beating for doing wrong and endure it? But if you suffer for doing good and you endure it, this is commendable before God.*

Key Observation. Even those of low status can choose to do good when threatened with suffering.

Understanding the Word. Slaves were everywhere in the first century. Some scholars estimate that slaves made up 25 percent of the population of the Roman Empire. Slavery in the empire was similar to and different from slavery in North America. In the ancient world people became slaves by being captured in war, by racking up debts they could not pay, and by being born into slavery. Slavery was not about race or color. Those who were slaves were at the bottom of the social ladder. Slaves were often viewed as children. They could not testify in trials. They were seen as liars and deceivers who could not be trusted. The elite used slaves for a variety of work, including cooking, cleaning, writing, managing businesses, farming, and other jobs. In addition, slaves could be sent to hard labor in the mines or rowing ships. Many who were sent to this type of work died within a year or two. Slaves were at the mercy of their masters and could be beaten, whipped, and abused at will. They were the property of those who owned them, and their lives were in the hands of their masters. Sometimes slaves could earn money running small business schemes, and it was possible for them to save money and buy their freedom. At other times, masters freed slaves after years of service. But freedom was not guaranteed. Freed slaves could not become citizens, and they continued to have low status in the community.

Peter sends instruction to the household slaves. The word for "slave" in verse 18 is different from the word for "slave" in verse 16. In verse 16 all Christians are referred to as God's slaves using the common word for any slave. In verse 18, the word specifically refers to household slaves. In other examples of a household code, there is usually an address to both masters and slaves (Ephesians 6:5–9; Colossians 3:22–4:1). But Peter uses the form of a household code and adapts it for his purposes. He only addresses the slaves. In addition, in the wider culture, discussions of household management were often addressed only to the men (for example, Aristotle's *Politics*). Peter addresses slaves as people who are capable of hearing instruction and choosing to live rightly. This was a shocking position in the first-century world.

In this context, where masters wielded absolute power over their slaves, Peter instructs slaves to submit to the authority of their masters. He goes on to indicate that if they suffer, such suffering should not be on account of sin.

If someone sins and is punished, that is justice. Instead, suffering on account of doing what is right in the eyes of God is good. No matter how their masters treat them, they are to pursue good. They are to act with integrity, honesty, and purity even in the face of evil. Throughout, they can be reminded that ultimately, they belong to God and answer to God, their true Master.

1. Have you ever suffered because you chose to do what is right in the eyes of God?

2. There are low-status Christians around the world who suffer because of their faith. How might they be an example for us today?

FOUR

Jesus Is Our Example

1 Peter 2:21–23 ESV *For to this you have been called, because Christ also suffered for you, leaving you an example, so that you might follow in his steps. 22He committed no sin, neither was deceit found in his mouth. 23When he was reviled, he did not revile in return; when he suffered, he did not threaten, but continued entrusting himself to him who judges justly.*

Key Observation. There is no greater example of unjust suffering than the example of Jesus.

Understanding the Word. When we think about the cross, we often think about what Jesus accomplished for us through his death. But Peter points our attention to the suffering of Jesus. And he reminds us that even though Jesus suffered, he did not sin. This is the example for all of us. We may do good works. We may live with integrity and honor. We may love others and live out our faith to the very best of our ability. And, we might still suffer *because of our faith.* Peter is not talking about the routine suffering that occurs in the lives of humanity—sickness, death, natural disasters, violence—he is talking about the suffering that Christians experience because they have lived out their faith in Jesus.

In light of such suffering, the call is to endure. The temptation would be to give up the activity that is bringing about one's suffering. For example, a slave might be required to give up worship, assembly with other Christians, and talking about Jesus. The challenge is to persist in Christian faith in the midst of opposition. This includes violent opposition such as the slaves might have experienced when being beaten because of their faith.

Jesus is the example to follow in such situations. In fact, the slaves are told they can follow in his footsteps. Jesus has led the way by not committing sin when he endured suffering. Since Peter's letter is designed to encourage the church to be holy (1:14–16), it is helpful to remind them that their leader, Jesus, demonstrated how to be holy in the midst of suffering. Jesus was fully human but did not sin. It can be tempting to look at Jesus and say, "Well, it was easy for him not to sin because he was God." But Jesus was fully human and was tempted as we are (Hebrews 2:18), and he did not sin. He was holy like his Father, and Peter invites his readers to follow in the footsteps of Jesus by also becoming holy (1 Peter 1:14–16). Jesus did not deceive. In the middle of suffering, the temptation is to do what Peter did on the night of Jesus' trial. Peter said, "I don't know him" (Luke 22:57). He used deceit and denial to avoid association with Jesus. But Jesus does not deceive in the face of suffering. When people mocked and abused Jesus, he did not return that abuse or threaten those who abused him. Instead, Jesus forgave those who crucified him (Luke 23:34). When Jesus was suffering, he entrusted himself to God. He committed himself to God's care. Jesus knew that God was a just judge (1 Peter 1:17), and he knew that he could trust God to act rightly and to see who was in the right. This gave him the confidence he needed when he was suffering to remain without sin. Jesus knew that God would be the ultimate Judge of both his own actions and the actions of those who abused him.

1. How does our scripture today encourage you to choose what is good and right even if you might face suffering for it?

2. What does it mean to you to entrust yourself to the one who judges justly?

FIVE

Jesus Restores

1 Peter 2:24–25 ESV *He himself bore our sins in his body on the tree, that we might die to sin and live to righteousness. By his wounds you have been healed. ²⁵For you were straying like sheep, but have now returned to the Shepherd and Overseer of your souls.*

Key Observation. Jesus' death on the cross enables us to live a new life in right relationship with God and others.

Understanding the Word. Peter addresses slaves directly and indicates that they have the power to choose to follow Jesus. They have the power to choose to act rightly even in the face of suffering. This is a distinctive use of the household code. The other distinctive feature of Peter's household code is that all the instructions are rooted in theology. Peter's reasons are not based on what is appropriate or reasonable in the culture. Instead, they are based on who God is and how God has acted through Jesus. God is the foundation of all the actions that the members of the household take. Peter's understanding of God is rooted in the Old Testament.

First Peter 2:22–25 is adapted from Isaiah 53:4–12. This chapter in Isaiah describes the Suffering Servant. He takes on the sins of Israel and experiences suffering on account of their transgressions. After his suffering God exalts him (Isaiah 53:12). Peter adapts material from this passage to describe the suffering and death of Jesus. The goal that Peter has set for the Christian community is to become holy as their Father is holy (1 Peter 1:14–16). How is that possible? It is made possible because Jesus carried our sins on the cross. The purpose of Jesus' death was to enable us to die to sin. Those who trust in Jesus are no longer slaves to sin. Instead, Jesus' death enables us to live to righteousness. This is what empowers believers to do good works and to live with honor and integrity. Christians do not generate this way of life from within themselves. Instead, this is a gift given to Christians by the power of Jesus' death on the cross.

Jesus' death on the cross enables new life—the same new life that was described as the new birth in 1 Peter 1:3. And it brings about healing. There are a lot of different images for sin in the Bible. Sometimes we think about sin as breaking the law or missing the mark. Another image for sin is sickness or disease. Jesus' death is able to heal us from the sickness of sin.

There are also many pictures of the church in the New Testament. In 1 Peter we already observed the church as God's household, God's temple, and God's priesthood. Now we see the church as a flock of sheep. These sheep were wandering. In other words, they were lost and in danger. But now, through the death of Jesus, they have returned. They are safe in the care of the Good Shepherd, who watches over them. The slaves who suffer because of unjust masters discover that God is their true shepherd. The slave who is despised by others receives the gift of new life from Jesus' death on his or her behalf. This gift from Jesus is the source of power for all right behavior in the face of suffering.

1. How are you learning to appropriate the power of Jesus' death to enable you to live well?

2. Have you experienced freedom from sin or have you experienced healing from the sickness of sin? Describe this and give thanks to the Shepherd who cares for you.

WEEK FOUR

GATHERING DISCUSSION OUTLINE

A. **Open session in prayer.** Ask that God would astonish us anew with fresh insight from God's Word and transform us into the disciples that Jesus desires us to become.

B. **Read 1 Peter 2:11–25 out loud.** You might consider having each member of the group read a verse or asking several people to each read three or four verses.

C. **View video for this week's readings.**

D. What were key insights or takeaways that you gained from your reading during the week and from watching the video commentary? In particular, how did these help you to grow in your faith and understanding of Scripture this week? What parts of the Bible lesson or study raised questions for you?

E. **One main point from this week is**: *As God's people, we are to live differently than the culture around us, honoring everyone, doing good works for those who are believers as well as those who are not, even if it brings about suffering for ourselves.*

F. **Discuss questions selected from the daily readings.**

1. **KEY OBSERVATION:** God's new family is called to good works.

   DISCUSSION QUESTION: Have you had an experience where you did the right thing (or a good deed), but it was misunderstood or even seen as evil by those around you?

2. **KEY OBSERVATION:** As God's servants, we should honor everyone.

   DISCUSSION QUESTION: Pick one or two of the last four commands (honor the emperor, love the brotherhood, fear God, honor everyone). How do we live that instruction in our world today?

3. **KEY OBSERVATION:** Even those of low status can choose to do good when threatened with suffering.

   DISCUSSION QUESTION: There are low-status Christians around the world who suffer because of their faith. How might they be an example for us today?

4. **KEY OBSERVATION:** There is no greater example of unjust suffering than the example of Jesus.

   DISCUSSION QUESTION: What does it mean to you to entrust yourself to the one who judges justly?

5. **KEY OBSERVATION:** Jesus' death on the cross enables us to live a new life in right relationship with God and others.

   DISCUSSION QUESTION: How are you learning to appropriate the power of Jesus' death to enable you to live well?

G. **As the study concludes, consider specific ways that this week's Bible lesson invites you to grow and calls you to change.** How do this week's scriptures call us to think differently? How do they challenge us to change in order to align ourselves with God's work in the world? What specific actions should we take to apply the insights of the lesson to our daily lives? What kind of person does our Bible lesson call us to become?

H. **Close session with prayer.** Emphasize God's ongoing work of transformation in our lives in preparation for loving mission and service in the world. Pray for missing class members as well as for people whom we need to invite to join our study.

1 Peter 3:1–12

Life in Society as God's Household: Part II

ONE

Preaching without Words

1 Peter 3:1–2 *Wives, in the same way submit yourselves to your own husbands so that, if any of them do not believe the word, they may be won over without words by the behavior of their wives, ²when they see the purity and reverence of your lives.*

Key Observation. Christians should let their behavior be so full of God's purity that others are drawn to the good news.

Understanding the Word. In this new section of the household code, Peter addresses wives. These women are married to husbands who do not believe in Jesus. In the context of marriage, the general expectation of first-century culture was that women would be obedient, faithful, and honorable in their actions. Women had gained a certain amount of freedom in the Roman Empire that allowed them to exercise some decisions about their marriages, money, and social engagement. But a good wife still attended to the needs of her husband and family as her primary responsibility. Plutarch, a first-century author, said, "A wife ought not to make friends on her own, but to enjoy her husband's friends in common with him. The gods are the first and most important friends. Wherefore it is becoming for a wife to worship and to know only the gods that her husband believes in, and to shut the front door tight upon

44

all queer rituals and outlandish superstitions."[2] A woman who followed Jesus while her husband did not found herself in a difficult situation. She had made friends with God and become a follower of Jesus Christ, a man who had been executed for crimes against the state.

Peter's advice to Christian wives is that they respect their husbands' authority. This does not mean slavish obedience to their husbands. They are not to obey every command that their husbands might issue. And this does not mean that women must stay in abusive relationships. Submission does not mean that those whose lives are in danger cannot flee from their abusers. Instead, it is a general respect for the authority of their husbands.

The wife is to act respectfully toward her husband and to submit to his direction in their family. Her actions have a purpose. The goal of her behavior is to win over her husband to the gospel. The woman is to be a silent evangelist. She is to proclaim the good news through her actions. And her actions are to be characterized by two particular attitudes. First, she is to live a life of moral purity. Once again, God calls on those who have been born again to live new lives. These lives are characterized by holiness. In particular, the wife should be faithful to her husband. There should be no reason for the husband to think that she is having an affair. The wife's actions should not call into question her purity.

The second attitude is reverence. Throughout 1 Peter, reverence is directed toward God. Ultimately, the wife of an unbeliever chooses to live as a quiet witness because of her relationship with God. Hopefully, her husband will see her reverence for God, and its impact on him may be a desire to know the God she worships. Although this portion of Scripture is addressed to wives, its call to purity and reverence are applicable to every follower of Jesus. The wives are an example to all.

1. In your most intimate relationships, what behaviors would most clearly communicate the gospel without using words?

2. In what way is your life already characterized by purity, and how can you grow in purity?

---

2. Plutarch, "Coniugalia Praecepta," *Moralia*, Loeb Classical Library ed. (1928; public domain), 2.19.

TWO

Inner Beauty

1 Peter 3:3–6 NRSV *Do not adorn yourselves outwardly by braiding your hair, and by wearing gold ornaments or fine clothing; ⁴rather, let your adornment be the inner self with the lasting beauty of a gentle and quiet spirit, which is very precious in God's sight. ⁵It was in this way long ago that the holy women who hoped in God used to adorn themselves by accepting the authority of their husbands. ⁶Thus Sarah obeyed Abraham and called him lord. You have become her daughters as long as you do what is good and never let fears alarm you.*

Key Observation. Unfading beauty comes from within.

Understanding the Word. The scripture today begins with a contrast between the external and the internal. Peter notes three types of outward adornment. Each of these types of adornment can be marks of beauty and of status. It is those with time and access to resources who are able to create elaborate hairstyles. There are statues and murals from the first century that show women with complicated braided hairstyles. Similarly, putting on gold and expensive clothing were also markers of high status. Peter does not prohibit this kind of attention to the outer person, but it is not to be the focus or emphasis for Christians. Instead, the real location of beauty is the inner person. True beauty consists of an interior life that is characterized by a spirit of gentleness and peace.

These two qualities are characteristics that all Christians should exemplify. In 1 Peter 3:15 we see that all Christians are to act with gentleness when defending their faith. The opposite of gentleness is harshness. Similarly, wives are to live quietly. While this may refer to their use of words, it can also refer to a general disposition of quietness. These inner characteristics reveal themselves in outward actions—the kinds of actions that help win unbelievers. First Peter 3:1–2 talks about the husbands who see the purity of their wives' lives. Now, 1 Peter 3:4 reminds wives that what matters most is that they are beautiful in the sight of God. As humans we are inclined to measure our worth by how others view us, but Peter reminds us that the interior life is what matters in the eyes of God.

Peter then points to two examples. First, godly women like Sarah, Rebekah, Rachel, and Leah lived this way in the past (v. 5). Second, he points more particularly to Sarah and her relationship with Abraham (v. 6). This last example is a little challenging. On the one hand, Sarah obeyed Abraham and her obedience caused her to suffer. For example, in Genesis 12:10–20 and Genesis 20 Abraham instructed Sarah to say that she was his sister. Both times, she was taken by the king of the land into his harem. And in Genesis 20:13 Abraham confesses that because he was afraid for his life, he has asked Sarah to say this everywhere they went. It is only after this confession that Sarah finally conceives the son of the promise, Isaac. But these stories do not explicitly say that Sarah called Abraham lord. Only in Genesis 18:12 does Sarah actually call Abraham lord. And there it seems that even though she laughs at the idea of bearing a child in her old age, she still refers to her husband with a term of respect. Christian wives who have experienced the new birth join in the covenant identity that Sarah shared with Abraham. Those who share in the new covenant identity of God's people are characterized by doing good and not being frightened even by things that cause fear. Once again, Peter plays out the logic of new birth. Those who are born again are made new and their behavior is also made new.

1. How has your inner self been made new through the new birth and cleansing work of God?

2. What does a life of gentleness and quietness look like for you?

THREE

Coheirs of Grace

1 Peter 3:7 NRSV *Husbands, in the same way, show consideration for your wives in your life together, paying honor to the woman as the weaker sex, since they too are also heirs of the gracious gift of life—so that nothing may hinder your prayers.*

Key Observation. Inconsiderate behavior toward others can impact your prayers.

Understanding the Word. This is the final section of the household code that is addressed to a particular group. This message is addressed to husbands. These are not the husbands of the wives that were addressed in 1 Peter 3:1–6. Those wives were married to unbelieving husbands. This word is addressed to husbands that are married to wives who are also believers. They are to live with them considerately. Both Romans and Jews idealized a harmonious home life, but the reality often involved the dominance of the husband over the wife. Peter does not give husbands any reason to exercise dominance or force over their wives.

Instead, the husband is to honor his wife. Honor is the defining value of the first century. Honor is showing respect or esteem toward others. All the other significant values of the first century flowed out of that one. One obtained honor by fulfilling one's social and civic responsibilities, by being a faithful religious person, and through one's family relationships. What is interesting here is that the husband is given the responsibility of making sure that his wife receives honor within the relationship. Although he could shame her as the "weaker sex," he is instructed to lift her up. Most likely, the reference to the wife as the "weaker sex" is an observation that women are generally not as strong as men. There were some within the culture who thought of women as being morally weaker than men, but in the context of 1 Peter that does not seem to be the meaning here. Instead, women are identified as equal heirs of the gracious gift of life. Both men and women are equal recipients of the new life available in Christ. In a culture that sometimes tried to limit the ability of women to receive inheritances, Peter identifies both genders as having an equal capacity for inheritance. The inheritance they receive has been identified in 1 Peter 1:4 as imperishable, unfading, and undefiled (NRSV).

The behavior of the husband toward his wife is explicitly tied to the outcome of his prayers. Peter makes it clear that failing to live well with one's wife presents the possibility that one's prayers will not be answered. God's willingness to respond to our prayers is connected to our behavior toward others. Here we might remember Jesus' comment that our forgiveness by God is tied to our forgiveness of others (Matthew 6:14–15). In other words, it is not unusual for our behavior and our relationship to God to be tied together.

Once again, the advice that is offered to husbands is relevant to other members of the community as well. On the one hand, Peter's instruction that men should honor their wives is extraordinary within his culture. On the other hand, he has already instructed the whole community that they should honor everyone (1 Peter 2:17). This is the general attitude that Christians are to have toward others whether a person is the emperor, a servant, or a wife. All are worthy of receiving honor.

1. How do you honor (treat with respect) those to whom you are closest?

2. What is most challenging about Peter's instruction to live together with others as coheirs of grace?

FOUR

Love One Another, Again

1 Peter 3:8–9 *Finally, all of you, be like-minded, be sympathetic, love one another, be compassionate and humble. ⁹Do not repay evil with evil or insult with insult. On the contrary, repay evil with blessing, because to this you were called so that you may inherit a blessing.*

Key Observation. We follow the pattern of Jesus by loving one another and resisting evil.

Understanding the Word. Peter has finished his specific messages to slaves, wives, and husbands. Now, he once again addresses the whole community. In verse 8 he lays out five important characteristics that the Christian community is to exhibit toward each other. These characteristics are general in nature. Peter does not tell us exactly *how* to live them out. That work is left to those who hear his letter. Instead, he lays out the general character of the Christian community. These five traits can be understood in pairs working toward the middle. Being like-minded and having humility are both about the disposition of the mind. Being sympathetic and compassionate are about the dispositions of the heart. And loving one another is at the center. As we consider the following virtues, we might also think about how Jesus exhibits these virtues.

Be like-minded—a Christian community becomes like-minded by their shared love of God. They share a similar outlook on the life they have received in Christ. Jesus had the same mind as God the Father. They were like-minded (John 5:19–20).

Be sympathetic and compassionate—a Christian community understands the suffering that those among them experience and reaches out to them with concern. Jesus felt compassion for others (Matthew 14:14).

Be humble—it is easier for us to understand humility when we contrast it with pride. Pride (in its negative sense) is self-oriented. It grasps after superior status or recognition. Humility is other-oriented and puts others first. When we understand humility in this way, we can see how Jesus often put others ahead of himself. Jesus is described as entering Jerusalem humbly on a donkey (Matthew 21:5) even though as the true King he would have had the right to be exalted.

Love one another—Peter has already instructed his audience to love one another with pure hearts (1:22–23) and to love the brotherhood (2:17). Here, he reiterates this instruction to love, to follow the pattern of Jesus. Jesus himself says that his followers will be known by the love they have for one another (John 15:12–17)

In verse 9 Peter lays out the way the Christian community is to respond to those outside the household of God. Like Jesus in 1 Peter 2:23, the Christian community does not return evil for evil or insult for insult. Instead, when someone does evil toward them, they return blessing. Christians do this because they have received the blessing of new life. Out of the blessing they have received, they offer blessing even to those who treat them cruelly. Blessing is treating others in ways that bring about the well-being of the other person. Sometimes the choice not to retaliate is a choice to endure suffering. This was the calling of the slaves in 1 Peter 2:21. All Christians are called to a life of blessing others and for some this may entail suffering.

1. Which of the first five characteristics do you find the easiest to identify in your own life? Which is the most difficult? What are some practical ways that you might demonstrate these characteristics to others in the Christian community?

2. How has your awareness of receiving blessing from God enabled you to bless others, even those who have mistreated you?

FIVE

Pursuing the Good Life

1 Peter 3:10–12 *For, "Whoever would love life and see good days must keep their tongue from evil and their lips from deceitful speech. ¹¹They must turn from evil and do good; they must seek peace and pursue it. ¹²For the eyes of the Lord are on the righteous and his ears are attentive to their prayer, but the face of the Lord is against those who do evil."*

Key Observation. The Lord is listening to the prayers of those who have good speech, do good for the community, and seek peace with others.

Understanding the Word. Peter rounds up his instructions to households with a quotation from Psalm 34. If you have a little extra time, take a few minutes to look up Psalm 34 and read the whole psalm. When you do, you'll notice several things. First, this psalm was written at a time when David was afraid for his life. King Saul was pursuing him, and David decided to flee to the enemy—the Philistines. However, they also considered David to be an enemy. So to escape, he pretended to be crazy (1 Samuel 21:13). Just as the audience of 1 Peter was struggling with life, so too David was facing challenges in his life. Second, this psalm is filled with good uses of speech. The mouth is to be used to praise and worship God and boast of the things that God has done. Third, ultimately this psalm declares, "The Lord is close to the brokenhearted and saves the crushed in spirit" (v. 18). The people who first heard 1 Peter knew the Old Testament well, and when Peter quoted from this psalm, other parts of the psalm would have echoed in their minds.

Peter chooses three verses from the psalm to sum up the household code. The first two verses restate the kind of behavior that Christians should have. The final verse focuses on God. The quotation begins by appealing to the desire to have a good, long life. Those who desire the good life must control their speech. In particular, they are to avoid evil speech and lying. We have already seen in the pattern of Jesus (2:21–25) and in the instructions to others that Christians are to avoid insulting, disparaging, abusing, or mistreating others with their words. And Christians are to be known as people who can be counted on to speak the truth and to avoid lying. Their good speech is to be matched with good behavior. They are to "do good." This refers back to loving one another and responding to each other with compassion and humility. How this works out in practice will vary from one circumstance to another. And they are to pursue peace. Here we might think of the peace that comes from dwelling together with like-minded others and not stirring up trouble among one's neighbors.

Finally, Peter reminds us that the Lord sees everything. He sees both the righteous and the wicked. The Lord is attentive to the prayers of those who are controlling their speech, doing good in the community, and seeking peace with others. But the Lord sets his face against those who do evil. Still, God stops short of destroying those who are evil because his ultimate desire is that those who oppose him also become part of his family.

1. As you think back through the household code (1 Peter 2:11–3:12— our last two weeks of study), what stands out to you about how the pattern of Jesus (2:21–25) is lived out by different groups of people in different circumstances?

2. Where do you see yourself being addressed within the household code?

3. What do you find most challenging about the call to control speech, do good in the community, and seek peace with others?

WEEK FIVE

GATHERING DISCUSSION OUTLINE

A. **Open session in prayer.** Ask that God would astonish us anew with fresh insight from God's Word and transform us into the disciples that Jesus desires us to become.

B. **Read 1 Peter 3:1–12 out loud.** You might consider having each member of the group read a verse or asking several people to each read three or four verses.

C. **View video for this week's readings.**

D. What were key insights or takeaways that you gained from your reading during the week and from watching the video commentary? In particular, how did these help you to grow in your faith and understanding of Scripture this week? What parts of the Bible lesson or study raised questions for you?

E. **One main point from this week is**: *Our inner life, as well as our behavior and words, can impact our prayers.*

F. **Discuss questions selected from the daily readings.**

1. **KEY OBSERVATION:** Christians should let their behavior be so full of God's purity that others are drawn to the good news.

DISCUSSION QUESTION: In your most intimate relationships, what behaviors would most clearly communicate the gospel without using words?

2. **KEY OBSERVATION:** Unfading beauty comes from within.

   DISCUSSION QUESTION: What does a life of gentleness and quietness look like for you?

3. **KEY OBSERVATION:** Inconsiderate behavior toward others can impact your prayers.

   DISCUSSION QUESTION: How do you honor (treat with respect) those whom you are the closest?

4. **KEY OBSERVATION:** We follow the pattern of Jesus by loving one another and resisting evil.

   DISCUSSION QUESTION: How has your awareness of receiving blessing from God enabled you to bless others, even those who have mistreated you?

5. **KEY OBSERVATION:** The Lord is listening to the prayers of those who have good speech, do good for the community, and seek peace with others.

   DISCUSSION QUESTION: What do you find most challenging about the call to control speech, do good in the community, and seek peace with others?

G. **As the study concludes, consider specific ways that this week's Bible lesson invites you to grow and calls you to change.** How do this week's scriptures call us to think differently? How do they challenge us to change in order to align ourselves with God's work in the world? What specific actions should we take to apply the insights of the lesson to our daily lives? What kind of person does our Bible lesson call us to become?

H. **Close session with prayer.** Emphasize God's ongoing work of transformation in our lives in preparation for loving mission and service in the world. Pray for missing class members as well as for people whom we need to invite to join our study.

1 Peter 3:13–4:2

Christians Follow the Suffering and Sovereign Lord

ONE

Suffering for Righteousness

1 Peter 3:13–14a ESV *Now who is there to harm you if you are zealous for what is good?* *¹⁴But even if you should suffer for righteousness' sake, you will be blessed.*

Key Observation. We are to be eager to do good deeds even if doing so brings about suffering.

Understanding the Word. Our study this week opens with a focus on the suffering that Christians may endure because of the good works they do as part of the life of faith. It closes with the example of Christ. Jesus also suffered, but God vindicated his suffering by raising him from death and seating him in the position of power at his right hand. This is the basis for our hope.

Many of us embrace the idea that if we do what is right, we will have a good life. This seems to be the idea behind the opening question in verse 13. If we are eager to do good, who is going to harm us for that? The expected answer is "no one." This verse about "doing good" and "harm" follows immediately after the quotation from Psalm 34 and helps connect this new section of the letter that focuses on suffering with the household code that came before. The quotation from Psalm 34 reminded us that God's eyes are on both the righteous and the wicked. Now, this is made more explicit. The righteous are those who are eager to do good works. The wicked are those who seek to do harm. Peter asks, "Who can harm you?" Ultimately even those who bring suffering cannot bring ultimate harm and destruction to Christians because God holds the lives of Christians in his hands.

In the next verse, Peter indicates that it is possible that his readers may experience suffering. Indeed, we have already seen suffering throughout 1 Peter (see 1:7; 2:11–12; 2:20). Here, Peter alludes to the words of Jesus in Matthew 5:10, "Blessed are those who are persecuted for righteousness' sake" (ESV). Blessing is the experience of receiving God's favor. Those who experience suffering on account of their faith have favor in the eyes of God. Peter is familiar with suffering for doing good deeds. In Acts 3–4 we read the story of a lame man who was healed by Peter as they entered the temple. At the end of Acts 3, Peter and his companions are arrested. The next day they are brought to trial, and Peter says this in court: "If we are being examined today concerning a good deed done to a crippled man . . ." (Acts 4:9). In other words, the good deed that Peter did and the resulting proclamation of God's healing and redemptive power were the very things that got him thrown into prison and dragged into court. When Peter indicates to the Christians in Asia Minor that doing good deeds may bring about suffering, he is reiterating the words of Jesus and his own personal experience.

As the family of God, we have been born anew. Our new birth sets us apart as God's people. We learn to live as the family of God in all spheres of life. And we become eager to do good deeds that reflect our family identity even if this brings about suffering.

1. Are you eager to do good deeds? What kind of good deeds are you doing?

2. Think about the different spheres of your life (family, friends, neighbors, coworkers, etc.). What kind of good deeds might you do in these different spheres?

TWO

Honor Christ as Holy

1 Peter 3:14b–16 ESV *Have no fear of them, nor be troubled, ¹⁵but in your hearts honor Christ the Lord as holy, always being prepared to make a defense to anyone who asks you for a reason for the hope that is in you; yet do it with gentleness and respect, ¹⁶having a good conscience, so that, when you are slandered, those who revile your good behavior in Christ may be put to shame.*

Key Observation. We are commanded to recognize that God is holy, to treasure that in our hearts, and to be prepared to share it with others.

Understanding the Word. Our reading today is one long complex sentence. We will unpack it together starting with the main instruction. The command is to honor Christ as holy, literally to set Christ apart in our hearts. Peter uses a quotation from Isaiah 8:12 to draw out this idea. In that context, Isaiah was instructing Israel not to be afraid of their enemies. Instead, they were to recognize the Lord's holiness and honor the Lord. Similarly, the people to whom Peter is writing to should not fear those who may persecute them and cause them suffering. Just like the people of Israel, they are to honor the Lord. But Peter does an amazing thing. Instead of just quoting Isaiah 8:12, he adds the title "Christ" to the word "Lord." By doing this he is making a statement about Jesus Christ. Christ is the Lord. Peter has already explored the relationship between God and Jesus. In 1:1–2 we see all the members of the godhead involved in the creation of God's new family. In 1:3 we see Jesus identified as the Son of God. And now, Jesus is identified as the Lord, the One whom they are to consecrate in their hearts.

Because they have set apart Christ in their hearts to honor him, they are able to defend the hope that they have within. Through their experience of new birth (their own initiation into the resurrection) they have experienced living hope that impacts their lives now. The resurrection of Jesus provides hope for the final defeat of death, sin, and the devil. They are to be prepared to offer a defense for their hope anytime they have the opportunity. That defense is to be done with a spirit of gentleness. This is the same attitude that was used to describe the wives in 3:4. The wives are a practical example of how to offer a defense of the good news in one particular circumstance. All Christians are to be prepared to offer a gentle defense of the good news whenever asked.

When they offer their defense, it is to be with a clear conscience. Their words and behavior must be acceptable in the sight of God. One is blessed if he or she suffers for righteousness (3:14) but not for sinful words or actions. The conscience must be clear before God. Then, when people say false things about your behavior or speech, they will be ashamed. Peter anticipates that his readers will experience suffering on account of their faith. People will say cruel, false, unpleasant things about others because of their Christian faith. But in the end, they will be put to shame. God will do the shaming. In the first-century world, "being put to shame" meant something like "being taken down a rung." In other words, the status of the person who is shamed is reduced.

1. When you think about the holiness of Jesus, what comes to mind and how do you treasure that in your heart?

2. How have you prepared yourself to present the good news about Jesus when asked?

3. What behaviors or types of speech are you exhibiting that would draw people to ask you about "the hope that is within you"?

THREE

Christ Suffered to Bring Us to God

1 Peter 3:17–20 ESV *For it is better to suffer for doing good, if that should be God's will, than for doing evil. ¹⁸For Christ also suffered once for sins, the righteous for the unrighteous, that he might bring us to God, being put to death in the flesh but made alive in the spirit, ¹⁹in which he went and proclaimed to the spirits in prison, ²⁰because they formerly did not obey, when God's patience waited in the days of Noah, while the ark was being prepared, in which a few, that is, eight persons, were brought safely through water.*

Key Observation. The crucified Christ suffered for sin to bring us to God. He was raised to life and proclaimed his triumph over sin, death, and evil.

Understanding the Word. Today and tomorrow we will be studying a passage that is very difficult. Some famous scholars have even said that they were not sure exactly what this passage is about (vv. 18–22). Despite that, there are some significant truths that we can uncover as we read and think carefully about this passage over the next couple of days. It is important to remember Peter's purpose. He is writing a letter of encouragement. So, as we explore these challenging verses, we will want to ask: In what way is this an encouraging message for people who are suffering?

Peter begins by restating a message that we have already seen several times (e.g., 2:20). Namely, let any persecution (suffering) you experience come about because of the good you are doing. Suffering at the hands of others should not be a result of doing evil. The reference to the will of God reminds the readers that they can entrust themselves to God's hands even when they experience suffering.

Peter reminds them that Jesus also suffered. In 2:21 Jesus' suffering was an example to the slaves. But in this verse his suffering is unique. Instead of being an example, it is the basis for our salvation. The one who was crucified ("put to death in the flesh") and resurrected ("made alive in the spirit") suffered on the cross. This only happened one time because only one sacrifice was required. This sacrifice cleanses us from sin and brings us to God. Jesus, the one truly good and righteous person, suffered on behalf of all of humanity. We were not good, but he suffered for our sins, so we can be reconciled to God.

After his resurrection Jesus went and preached to the spirits in prison (v. 19). There are *many* opinions about what this means. Following a number of scholars, I think that after his ascension Jesus proclaimed his victory over sin and death to fallen angels (spirits). There are hints in the Bible about these fallen angels. Genesis 6:1–3 (the narrative immediately before the Noah story) and Jude 6 both mention them. Popular literature at the time of Jesus also told stories about these fallen angels. These angels rebelled against (disobeyed) God's rule in heaven and sought to rule in the place of God. They were defeated and cast out of heaven. Jesus proclaimed their full and final defeat.

God is described as one who waits patiently as a means of escape, the ark, is built. When the ark was built, judgment came. Then, Noah and his family were saved from the flood. The ark carried them safely. And their salvation was through water. This mention of "salvation through water" will connect to our lesson tomorrow, where we will read about baptism. These verses encourage those who are suffering persecution to remember that Jesus has won the victory over evil.

1. How is this passage a word of encouragement for those suffering for their faith?

2. How does Christ's suffering on the cross relate to your own experience of forgiveness, healing, or rescue?

F O U R

Jesus Reigns

1 Peter 3:21–22 *and this water symbolizes baptism that now saves you also—not the removal of dirt from the body but the pledge of a clear conscience toward God. It saves you by the resurrection of Jesus Christ, ²²who has gone into heaven and is at God's right hand—with angels, authorities and powers in submission to him.*

Key Observation. Jesus, the One who reigns, enables us to make our pledge to God in baptism.

Understanding the Word. Verses 21–22 are the end of a long complex sentence that began in verse 18. Baptism corresponds to the picture of Noah that was described in verse 20. Noah and his family were saved in a boat that brought them to safety. The allusions to Noah's rescue from destruction and to the water remind Peter of baptism. In the days of Noah, the water of the flood was destructive to those who did not believe. But to those who believed it became part of the way they were saved. The boat floated on the water. Now Peter points to the water as a symbol of baptism.

What is baptism? Peter wants to make it very clear that baptism is not about taking a bath or washing oneself in a ceremonial way. There is no particular prescription for immersion or sprinkling or for the amount of water that is used, because ultimately baptism is not about external cleansing. Instead, baptism is about the relationship between God and his people. In baptism, a person makes a pledge to God. With baptism, then, we are demonstrating our commitment to the one who has given us new birth. Pledges were a part of the baptismal practice of the early church, and by the second century the church saw baptism as a formal commitment. The pledge made before God demonstrates awareness of God's will. And it is a commitment to the life of holiness that God calls his family to exhibit.

Baptism alone is not a means of salvation. Instead, it is the resurrection of Jesus Christ that gives baptism its saving force. Peter has already explained in the book that salvation is initiated out of God's mercy and is experienced as new birth (1:3). He has shown that the sacrifice of Jesus is a key component of our liberation from bondage (1:18). And he has made it clear that our healing from sin depends on the Suffering Servant, who bears sin on our behalf on the cross. So, here he can briefly mention the mechanism of the resurrection as one more piece of God's saving work. Baptism is the outward sign of the pledge one makes to God to live in line with God's will.

First Peter 3:18–19 began with Jesus' suffering and death. Verse 22 ends with Jesus' journey into the presence of God (heaven) and his position at the right hand of God. Jesus is located in the position of power in heaven. And he is depicted with angels, authorities, and powers in submission to him. In other words, in our passage Jesus goes from suffering (v. 18) to triumph (v. 22). This is a great word of encouragement for our audience, who are experiencing suffering because of their faith. First, they are reminded that Christ's suffering, death, and resurrection bring them new life. Second, they are reminded that Christ has triumphed over death and those who sought to destroy him. Likewise, they can anticipate that even though they suffer for their faith, Jesus will vindicate them as they move forward in faithfulness.

1. If you have been baptized, how does thinking about baptism as a pledge impact your understanding of your baptism? If you have not been baptized, are you ready to make a pledge before God as a response to God's saving work on your behalf?

2. How does the triumph of Christ encourage you to continue living faithfully and witnessing to those around you?

FIVE

Think like Jesus

1 Peter 4:1–2 ESV *Since therefore Christ suffered in the flesh, arm yourselves with the same way of thinking, for whoever has suffered in the flesh has ceased from sin, ²so as to live for the rest of the time in the flesh no longer for human passions but for the will of God.*

Key Observation. In the midst of suffering, we are to have the mind of Christ and live out the will of God for our lives.

Understanding the Word. Peter has moved through the suffering, death, resurrection, and triumphant ascension of Jesus in 3:18–22. Now Peter uses the word "therefore" to connect his argument in 4:1 to the previous verses *and* to indicate how Christians should live in light of that. He returns to the theme of suffering. This theme was first introduced in chapter 1 and is then followed up on more extensively in 2:18–25 and 3:13–18. The theme of suffering will continue in 4:1–6 and 4:12–19. Peter also returns to the idea that Christ's suffering serves as an example for Christians (1 Peter 2:21).

Once again Peter states that Jesus truly experienced physical suffering in his body. Because of this, Christians are to arm themselves with the same way of thinking as Jesus. The metaphor "arm yourselves" is drawn from the military context. It reminds us that Christians should be prepared for the hostile context in which they may live. The defense that Christians are to take up is a way of thinking like Christ. More particularly, this relates to having the same type of intention and purpose that Christ had. Throughout 1 Peter we have seen such things as meekness, not returning evil for evil, not slandering others when they slander you, and entrusting one's self to God as the kind of thinking that controls Jesus' action. Christians are encouraged to take up that same kind of thinking as a way of life in the midst of hostile people.

Peter goes on to say that the one who has suffered in the flesh has ceased from sin. Sin refers to activities that go against the will of God. The audience of 1 Peter has turned away from sinful activities (these will be discussed further in 4:4) and has turned their attention to God. They are growing in holiness and love for one another. These activities are replacing the sinful activities that characterized their life before new birth and redemption.

However long Christian have left before they die or the Lord returns, they are not to live according to ungodly desires. Here, we might think about 1:14 with its description of pre-conversion life as one characterized by "ignorant desires." Or, of 2:11 with its description of desires of the flesh that wage war against the soul. They are no longer to give their time to such things. Instead, the time remaining is to be given over to living in accordance with God's will. They already know what God's will is for their life. Namely, to become more and more like the one who gave them new birth—to become holy as God is holy.

1. How is Jesus an example for you in the midst of challenging circumstances? Describe practical ways that you can "arm yourself" so that you have the same disposition and intention as Jesus.

2. In what ways has it been hard to leave the old desires and have a heart in tune with God's will that you grow in holiness?

WEEK SIX

GATHERING DISCUSSION OUTLINE

A. **Open session in prayer.** Ask that God would astonish us anew with fresh insight from God's Word and transform us into the disciples that Jesus desires us to become.

B. **Read:** 1 Peter 3:13–4:2. You might consider having each member of the group read a verse or asking several people to each read three or four verses.

C. **View video for this week's readings.**

D. What were key insights or takeaways that you gained from your reading during the week and from watching the video commentary? In particular, how did these help you to grow in your faith and understanding of Scripture this week? What parts of the Bible lesson or study raised questions for you?

E. **One main point from this week is**: *As followers of Jesus, we are called to honor him and to grow into agreement with his mind and will. As he did, we will suffer along the way.*

F. **Discuss questions selected from the daily readings.**

1. **KEY OBSERVATION:** We are to be eager to do good deeds even if doing so brings about suffering.

    DISCUSSION QUESTION: Think about the different spheres of your life (family, friends, neighbors, coworkers, etc.). What kind of good deeds might you do in these different spheres?

2. **KEY OBSERVATION:** We are commanded to recognize that God is holy, to treasure that in our hearts, and to be prepared to share it with others.

   DISCUSSION QUESTION: How have you prepared yourself to present the good news about Jesus when asked?

3. **KEY OBSERVATION:** The crucified Christ suffered for sin to bring us to God. He was raised to life and proclaimed his triumph over sin, death, and evil.

   DISCUSSION QUESTION: How does Christ's suffering on the cross relate to your own experiences of forgiveness, healing, or rescue?

4. **KEY OBSERVATION:** Jesus, the One who reigns, enables us to make our pledge to God in baptism.

   DISCUSSION QUESTION: How does the triumph of Christ encourage you to continue living faithfully and witnessing to those around you?

5. **KEY OBSERVATION:** In the midst of suffering, we are to have the mind of Christ and live out the will of God for our lives.

   DISCUSSION QUESTION: In what ways has it been hard to leave the old desires and have a heart in tune with God's will that you grow in holiness?

G. **As the study concludes, consider specific ways that this week's Bible lesson invites you to grow and calls you to change.** How do this week's scriptures call us to think differently? How do they challenge us to change in order to align ourselves with God's work in the world? What specific actions should we take to apply the insights of the lesson to our daily lives? What kind of person does our Bible lesson call us to become?

H. **Close session with prayer.** Emphasize God's ongoing work of transformation in our lives in preparation for loving mission and service in the world. Pray for missing class members as well as for people whom we need to invite to join our study.

1 Peter 4:3–19

In the Midst of Suffering, Continue in Love and Joy

ONE

God's Horizon

1 Peter 4:3–6 *For you have spent enough time in the past doing what pagans choose to do—living in debauchery, lust, drunkenness, orgies, carousing and detestable idolatry. ⁴They are surprised that you do not join them in their reckless, wild living, and they heap abuse on you. ⁵But they will have to give account to him who is ready to judge the living and the dead. ⁶For this is the reason the gospel was preached even to those who are now dead, so that they might be judged according to human standards in regard to the body, but live according to God in regard to the spirit.*

Key Observation. Those who no longer participate in the pleasures of this world may suffer for that choice, but God will vindicate them.

Understanding the Word. We begin our study this week in the middle of a paragraph that describes the suffering faced both by Christ and his followers (4:1–6). Our study this week will weave together and expand on two themes that we have seen earlier in 1 Peter—suffering and right behavior in the Christian community.

In 1 Peter 4:3–4 we see the kinds of activities in which the pagans around our audience choose to engage. We can sum up the list this way: wild partying and the worship of other gods. In first-century culture, festivals and feast days centered on the temples and shrines that filled the cities of Asia Minor. The types of wild behavior described could be part of the celebrations at the local temples. This behavior was not limited to the public sphere. Homes could also be the location of drunken parties, sexual license, and other ungodliness. Peter reminds his audience that they have experienced a new life and no longer participate in these types of activities. However, those around the Christians are surprised that they don't join in the same activities that they used to participate in. Their surprise turns to insults, abuse, and mockery (v. 4).

Once again Peter reminds Christians that there is a horizon beyond the here and now. In 1 Peter we have come to see that God is the Creator of the world and that Jesus and his redemptive work were known before the world began (1:20). We have also been reminded that Christ will return (1:7; 2:12) and that those who have mocked Christians will glorify God (2:23). Here, Peter reminds Christians that God judges both the living and the dead—both Christians and their persecutors will have to give an account before the throne of God.

First Peter 4:6 is another complicated verse that has been understood in a variety of ways. But in context, it seems that some who heard the good news had died. In the early church many expected that Jesus would return before they died. So a question arose about what happened to Christians who died. Verse 6 may relate to that question and reassures those who have suffered.

Some who heard the good news had died and experienced the judgment that happens to all of humanity. The sin of Adam and Eve brought about death as the consequence of sin. However, those who have heard and responded to the gospel find life after death in the spirit. This parallels the description of Jesus' death in 3:18. His crucifixion is described as "being put to death in the flesh," and his resurrection is described as "being made alive in the spirit." So, too, those who experience new birth in this life may still experience physical death. But they also anticipate resurrection and life in the Spirit in the age to come.

1. Have you given up behaviors that others in our world consider normal because of your Christian convictions? How have your unbelieving friends reacted to the choices you have made?

2. How does your belief in life after death and in God's judgment give you hope and impact the choices you make now?

T W O

Love One Another, Again

1 Peter 4:7–9 *The end of all things is near. Therefore be alert and of sober mind so that you may pray. ⁸Above all, love each other deeply, because love covers over a multitude of sins. ⁹Offer hospitality to one another without grumbling.*

Key Observation. The end is close at hand, so be clearheaded in order to pray. Love is the most important virtue of the church.

Understanding the Word. Once again, Peter reminds his audience that the world as they know it will come to an end. They should not place their trust in the material world. They must remember that there will be a day when the full plan and purpose of God will be revealed. Evil will be judged, and the glory of God will be revealed. Christians wait for and anticipate that day as if it is right around the corner.

Peter then goes on to give instructions about how to live in light of the end. As he has done throughout the book, Peter moves from a sentence or two of theological truth ("The end of all things is near") to action. Unlike what we see in some contemporary apocalyptic movies, there is no panic or fear. Instead, the lives of believers are characterized by wakeful soberness. This does not mean that Christians are grim, stern, or sour, and it does not mean that they do not experience joy or celebration. Here, sober refers to being clearheaded. It is the opposite of being drunk. The purpose of being clearheaded and attentive is so that we can pray well. We are enabled to see well so that we can pray for God's favor, God's intervention in our world, and God's forgiveness.

For the fourth time in this letter, Peter instructs his audience to love one another (1:22; 2:17; 3:8). Their love is to be deep. This refers to the ability to persevere in love with one another. People, even Christians, are sometimes difficult to love. But the instruction to the community is to persist in love. The reason they are to persist in love is because doing so covers a multitude of sins.

Scholars sometimes debate whose sin love covers. In other words, does the one who sinned have his or her sins covered? Or, does the one who forgives have his or her sins covered? But I think that it is more helpful to think about this from a community perspective. When the primary motive of Christians is to love one another and when they go out of their way to demonstrate their love for each other, the Christian community will flourish. God is delighted when his children live out of love toward one another.

Another practical way to show love in the community is to practice hospitality. The Greek word for hospitality is a compound word composed of the two words "love" and "stranger." Christians relied on hospitality from each other when they traveled, and it was to be given without grumbling. First-century households were larger than our own, and providing a bed and a meal were a way of welcoming a fellow believer. However, the traveler was not to take advantage of the host. In other early Christian texts, it is suggested that a three-day stay is long enough (*Didache* 12:1–2).

1. What does it look like to go out of your way to love a fellow Christian who has sinned against you? What do you hope will happen to you and to the other person if you persist in loving that individual?

2. How can you show hospitality to others in your own life?

THREE

God Supplies, We Serve

1 Peter 4:10–11 NASB *As each one has received a special gift, employ it in serving one another as good stewards of the manifold grace of God. [11] Whoever speaks, is to do so as one who is speaking the utterances of God; whoever serves is to do so as one who is serving by the strength which God supplies; so that in all things God may be glorified through Jesus Christ, to whom belongs the glory and dominion forever and ever. Amen.*

Key Observation. Christians are invited to be stewards of the gifts that God gives. As stewards, they are to serve one another.

Understanding the Word. This passage introduces us to the economy of God. God's economy begins with the gifts that God gives and we receive. What we have comes from God. We are invited to be stewards of the gifts we have received. A steward was a servant who managed the household interests for the head of the household. As those who have received gifts, we are invited into a position where we are given responsibility as one of God's managers. At the same time, we are God's servants too. Good stewards look out for the best interests of their master and seek to manage the resources that are entrusted to them for the benefit of the one who gave them. The head of our household instructs us to use the gifts he has given to serve each other.

We are entrusted with the "manifold grace of God." "Manifold" means various, and this reminds us that each of us receives different gifts. When we share them with one another, the whole church is strengthened and encouraged.

Peter speaks specifically of two gifts. The first one is the gift of speaking and the second is the gift of serving. In Paul, we are given several long lists of gifts (1 Corinthians 12:4–11; Ephesians 4:11), but Peter focuses on just two. These two gifts that Peter focuses on are gifts that everyone can receive and everyone can use. Each one of us has the capacity to speak divinely appointed words into the lives of others and to use the strength that God has given us to serve others.

Those who speak are to speak as one who is speaking the words of God. The words of God refer to Scripture and prophetic words that encourage the church and bring hope-filled truth. We learn what the words of God look like by attending to the significance of divine words in Scripture. This includes paying attention to the sayings of Jesus and their message for the church today.

Those who serve are able to do so because God supplies the strength we need for that service. Our service to others is never generated out of ourselves. Instead, it comes from God. We can rely on him to provide for us. And out of God's supply we can share with others and strengthen them.

The purpose of speaking and serving is so that God may be glorified through Jesus Christ. As good stewards, our faithful management of the gifts that God gives ultimately brings honor and praise and fame to God. Just as God shares gifts with us, so, too, God shares his glory with Jesus. Ultimately, Jesus will have dominion over all things into eternity. This is the one to whom we belong. Peter finishes this major unit (2:11–4:11) with a brief burst of praise to God and Jesus and a reminder that God is worthy of honor.

1. How are you stewarding the gifts that God has given you?

2. How are you speaking the words of God to others and serving others out of what God has supplied to you?

FOUR

Sharing Christ's Sufferings

1 Peter 4:12–14 NRSV *Beloved, do not be surprised at the fiery ordeal that is taking place among you to test you, as though something strange were happening to you. ¹³But rejoice insofar as you are sharing Christ's sufferings, so that you may also be glad and shout for joy when his glory is revealed. ¹⁴If you are reviled for the name of Christ, you are blessed, because the spirit of glory, which is the Spirit of God, is resting on you.*

Key Observation. Experiencing persecution because of one's faith is a normal part of the Christian life. God blesses those who suffer for him.

Understanding the Word. Today we begin looking at the last major section of 1 Peter (4:12–5:11). In this section Peter will revisit the problem of suffering that his audience is experiencing (4:12–19), and he will give further practical instructions to the church (5:1–11). Both of these sections continue familiar themes in the book. The setting in which the book takes place is life as resident aliens in the midst of a hostile culture. This results in suffering. But the instructions are the same. Pursue holiness.

As he did in 2:11, Peter uses a term of endearment for his audience: "Beloved." Their experience of suffering is described as a "fiery ordeal." This suffering could include verbal attacks, loss of jobs and resources, accusations and trials because of one's allegiance to Jesus, imprisonment, or on rare occasions martyrdom. As Christians, they should not be surprised when they suffer on account of their faith. It is not strange to suffer on account of one's Christian faith. Indeed, earlier in 1 Peter, it is clear that Jesus himself suffered and died. Christians can look to Jesus as an example of a person who suffers for being righteous before God.

Not only should they not be surprised, the attitude that they should have is one of rejoicing when they have the experience of sharing in Christ's sufferings. Christians are not to react to suffering for their faith in a way that they would be ashamed to own when they see Jesus face-to-face. Instead, they are to react in such a way that when they see Jesus they will be able to respond with gladness and joy. There will come a day when Jesus' full power and glory will be revealed, and Christians are to respond to persecution in a way that anticipates that end.

The words of 4:14 are reminiscent of the words that Jesus spoke in the Sermon on the Mount. "Blessed are you when people revile you and persecute you and utter all kinds of evil against you falsely on my account. Rejoice and be glad, for your reward is great in heaven, for in the same way they persecuted the prophets who were before you" (Matt. 5:11–12 NRSV). God's favor (blessing) rests on those who experience suffering for his name. The apostles themselves experienced this when they were imprisoned, beaten, and tried because of the name of Jesus (see Acts 4:5–22; 14:21–23). The second blessing in this passage is attached to suffering for the name of Christ, God's anointed one. Those who suffer in this way have the spirit of glory resting on them. This saying reminds me of Stephen, the first martyr, whose face glowed like an angel when he shared the good news about Jesus (Acts 6:15). When we are bold for Jesus (not to further ourselves or our projects), God's Spirit blesses that.

1. How does learning that suffering for one's faith is a normal part of the Christian life deepen your faith?

2. Name some examples of people who have suffered for their faith (these could be people from the Bible, from the history of the church, or from our contemporary setting). How have you seen God's blessing through them?

FIVE

Entrust Yourself to God

1 Peter 4:15–19 NRSV *But let none of you suffer as a murderer, a thief, a criminal, or even as a mischief maker. ¹⁶Yet if any of you suffers as a Christian, do not consider it a disgrace, but glorify God because you bear this name. ¹⁷For the time has come for judgment to begin with the household of God; if it begins with us, what will be the end for those who do not obey the gospel of God? ¹⁸And "If it is hard for the righteous to be saved, what will become of the ungodly and the sinners?" ¹⁹Therefore, let those suffering in accordance with God's will entrust themselves to a faithful Creator, while continuing to do good.*

Key Observation. Suffering should come about because of a Christian's godly life of faith and not because of sinful choices.

Understanding the Word. Peter continues to discuss the theme of suffering on account of one's faith. He reminds his audience that God does not approve of suffering that takes place because of wrongdoing. This is similar to the instructions that Peter gave to the slaves in the household (2:18–20). If slaves experienced suffering, that suffering should come about because of their godly lives. Being beaten as a slave for doing wrong was not looked on favorably by God. Similarly, suffering because one has committed a crime, such as murder or stealing, or suffering because one is a criminal or a mischief maker is not approved by God. But suffering because one is a Christian brings favor with God.

The word "Christian" was first used to describe followers of Jesus in Antioch (Acts 11:26). What began as a form of insult became a self-identification that those who followed Jesus claimed for themselves. "Christian" became the name of those who align themselves with Jesus. In a culture that places a heavy value on being an honorable person, being associated with Jesus and his generally poor band of followers could be the basis for shame and disgrace. But instead of being ashamed, they are to give glory to God that they are allowed to bear this name, Christian. It is the honor of the followers of Jesus to bear this insult and to bear it in such a way that God receives the glory.

Peter returns to the end-time horizon with the idea that judgment begins now with the family of God, the place where God dwells. One scholar puts it this way: "Present suffering . . . is the first act of final judgment."[3] It is uncommon to see the persecution of the godly as the beginning of judgment, but that is how Peter portrays it. He quickly moves on from this statement to a question. We might read that question like this: If our suffering as Christians is as shameful and difficult as it is, what will it be like for those who are not Christians? In the question, he gets at the idea that Christians are suffering greatly, but that the suffering of non-Christians when they encounter God's judgment will be worse.

This is followed by a quotation from Proverbs 11:31. We are reminded again that in 1 Peter salvation begins with new birth and ends at the revelation of Jesus Christ. It is a process that takes place over time. It is not easy, not even for those who are growing in holiness. But what is difficult for those who are becoming more and more like their Father—the Holy One—is outside the bounds of possibility for those who hear the good news and reject the message and the messenger.

Just as Jesus entrusted himself to God when he faced suffering (2:23), so, too, Christians can entrust their lives to the one who made them. God is faithful.

1. How have you grown in your experience of salvation (new birth, deliverance, reconciliation, and hope) over time?

2. How do you feel about identifying yourself as a Christian? What is comfortable or uncomfortable about being known as a Christian?

---

3. Lewis R. Donelson, *I & II Peter and Jude: A Commentary* (Louisville: Westminster John Knox, 2010), 138.

WEEK SEVEN

GATHERING DISCUSSION OUTLINE

A. **Open session in prayer.** Ask that God would astonish us anew with fresh insight from God's Word and transform us into the disciples that Jesus desires us to become.

B. **Read:** 1 Peter 4:3–19. You might consider having each member of the group read a verse or asking several people to each read three or four verses.

C. **View video for this week's readings.**

D. What were key insights or takeaways that you gained from your reading during the week and from watching the video commentary? In particular, how did these help you to grow in your faith and understanding of Scripture this week? What parts of the Bible lesson or study raised questions for you?

E. **One main point from this week is:** *Choose God and his holiness, and have no fear of the suffering it might bring.*

F. **Discuss questions selected from the daily readings.**

    1. **KEY OBSERVATION:** Those who no longer participate in the pleasures of this world may suffer for that choice, but God will vindicate them.

    DISCUSSION QUESTION: Have you given up behaviors that others in our world consider normal because of your Christian convictions? How have your unbelieving friends reacted to the choices you have made?

2. **KEY OBSERVATION:** The end is close at hand, so be clearheaded in order to pray. Love is the most important virtue of the church.

   DISCUSSION QUESTION: How can you show hospitality to others in your own life?

3. **KEY OBSERVATION:** Christians are invited to be stewards of the gifts that God gives. As stewards, they are to serve one another.

   DISCUSSION QUESTION: How are you stewarding the gifts God has given you?

4. **KEY OBSERVATION:** Experiencing persecution because of one's faith is a normal part of the Christian life. God blesses those who suffer for him.

   DISCUSSION QUESTION: Name some examples of people who have suffered for their faith (these could be people from the Bible, from the history of the church, or from our contemporary setting). How have you seen God's blessing through them?

5. **KEY OBSERVATION:** Suffering should come about because of a Christian's godly life of faith and not because of sinful choices.

   DISCUSSION QUESTION: How have you grown in your experience of salvation (new birth, deliverance, reconciliation, and hope) over time?

G. **As the study concludes, consider specific ways that this week's Bible lesson invites you to grow and calls you to change.** How do this week's scriptures call us to think differently? How do they challenge us to change in order to align ourselves with God's work in the world? What specific actions should we take to apply the insights of the lesson in our daily lives? What kind of person does our Bible lesson call us to become?

H. **Close session with prayer.** Emphasize God's ongoing work of transformation in our lives in preparation for loving mission and service in the world. Pray for missing class members as well as for people whom we need to invite to join our study.

1 Peter 5:1–14

Final Thoughts on the Life of the Church

ONE

Shepherding God's Flock

1 Peter 5:1–4 ESV *So I exhort the elders among you, as a fellow elder and a witness of the sufferings of Christ, as well as a partaker in the glory that is going to be revealed: ²shepherd the flock of God that is among you, exercising oversight, not under compulsion, but willingly, as God would have you; not for shameful gain, but eagerly; ³not domineering over those in your charge, but being examples to the flock. ⁴And when the chief Shepherd appears, you will receive the unfading crown of glory.*

Key Observation. Peter identifies himself as a leader and urges leaders in the church to care for God's flock.

Understanding the Word. In this final chapter of the letter, Peter continues his theme of living holy lives even in the midst of challenges. Now, he will address what that looks like for leaders, for younger believers, and for the whole congregation. Overall, he will stress the need for humility and alertness in the midst of a hostile situation. The letter concludes with greetings and a closing word of praise.

Peter identifies himself as a fellow elder, a leader in the church. He is also someone who testifies to the sufferings of Christ. Although Peter was not present at the cross, he saw the rejection, abuse, and humiliation that

Jesus suffered at various points in his ministry. And throughout his apostolic ministry, Peter testified to the crucifixion and death of Jesus. Those to whom he writes are now experiencing the suffering of Christ when they encounter persecution on account of the name of Jesus. Finally, Peter recognizes that he will come to share in the glory of God that will be revealed (cf. 1 Peter 1:7).

Leaders are to take care of the people of God as a shepherd takes care of sheep. This means that they are looking out for God's people, protecting them from danger, providing them with good food and water, and helping them to flourish. The people that the leaders care for belong to God. They are God's flock. Leaders have authority over the flock, but they are not to use that authority for their own benefit. It is okay for leaders to be paid for their work (1 Corinthians 3:8). But a leader should not be motivated by the possibility that they will gain money or wealth ("shameful gain") from those they lead. Leaders are to lead willingly and eagerly. Good shepherds do not dominate their sheep. Rather, they guide them. Good shepherds do not exploit their sheep. The prophet Ezekiel paints a picture of bad leaders who destroy the flock by using all the wool, eating the fat sheep, failing to heal the sick, and leaving those who stray vulnerable to predators (Ezekiel 34). Instead of preying on the sheep, good leaders live in such a way that those who follow them can model their lives after them.

Ultimately, the flock belongs to God. And the Chief Shepherd, Jesus, will return. Peter has reminded his audience of Jesus' return from the very beginning (1:7), and he continues to set that expectation before them. When Jesus returns, he will reward those who have cared well for the flock he left in their care. That reward will be unfading. The same word was used to describe their unfading inheritance that is kept in heaven (1:5). These are the true treasures that will never perish. They will also share in the glory (the amazing holy weight and light of God) that will be revealed at the last day.

1. When you are asked to lead within the context of the church, are you able to respond willingly and eagerly?

2. Share some examples of leaders you have known whose lives present a model of godly living to their followers. Are you living in such a way that your life can be an example for others?

T W O

Wear Humility

1 Peter 5:5 ESV *Likewise, you who are younger, be subject to the elders. Clothe yourselves, all of you, with humility toward one another, for "God opposes the proud but gives grace to the humble."*

Key Observation. The whole church is to practice humility toward one another.

Understanding the Word. Today our churches have a wide variety of leadership structures. Some have pastors with elders who oversee the pastor and the church. Some have pastors who report to a bishop. And others have a pastor who reports to the whole congregation. There are other structures as well. In the early church, leadership structures were still being developed. And Peter has just finished giving instructions about how the leaders of the church were to treat those they had authority over. It seems clear from 1 Peter that an elder was someone who gave guidance and care to the church. Those who were younger were to submit to the elders. The term "younger" here might mean either younger in the faith or younger in age. In either case, they are to give deference to the elders.

We have seen this structure before. In 2:18–3:7 Peter addressed three different groups (slaves, wives, and husbands) with directions that were relevant to their particular situation. But he allowed the whole church to listen in, so that they too could learn from those instructions. Once again, Peter is addressing two different groups (the elders and the younger ones) and allowing the church to listen in and learn from these two groups.

The household code in 1 Peter 2:11–3:12 began and ended with instructions addressed to the whole group (2:11–17 and 3:8–12). In the same way, Peter ends this set of instructions with direction to the whole church. They are to put on humility. This is the same virtue that is listed in 3:8 to describe the way we are to think of one another.

What is humility? Humility is a virtue that involves not thinking too highly of one's self. We can look to Jesus as the ultimate example of humility. Even though he was God he became a servant to humanity. He humbled himself to the point of death on a cross (Philippians 2:6–8). He did not think too much

79

of himself, and that allowed him to take on a lowly position in order to serve others. In a similar way, we should not think too much of ourselves or worry about what others think of us. Instead, we are concerned with God's opinion of us. Humility enables us to take up service toward others, and we can see them as God sees them. We are freed from our fear of being judged by others and assisted in treating them as fellow children of god.[4] We are free to speak the loving truth out of humble service to others. Humility comes out of deep and close relationship with God. It grows as we draw closer to the Holy One, who gives us new life. The whole church is to have this attitude toward one another. Both leaders and followers are to wear humility. This brings about mutual service and support in the context of the family of God. God opposes pride but gives his good gifts to the humble. For more on pride and humility, review Week 5, Day Four.

1. Does worrying about what others will think of you keep you from wholeheartedly responding to God's call to humble service?

2. In what ways can we practice humility in our own discipleship?

3. What examples of humility have you encountered, and how have they affected you?

THREE

He Cares for You

1 Peter 5:6–7 ESV *Humble yourselves, therefore, under the mighty hand of God so that at the proper time he may exalt you, [7]casting all your anxieties on him, because he cares for you.*

Key Observation. Our lives are in God's control, and he cares for us.

Understanding the Word. "Therefore" connects verses 6–7 with our material from yesterday. The shared attitude of the members of God's family is one

---

4. Jon Bloom, "Humility Is Not Always Nice," *Desiring God*, June 3, 2016, https://www .desiringgod.org/articles/humility-is-not-always-nice.

of humility. God extends his grace to the humble. God's grace is a free gift. Grace is the gifts and favor of God that he extends to us. It is not earned or deserved. Instead it is received with open hands. Having open rather than grasping hands is one way to demonstrate humility. When we have open hands, we have a disposition to receive with trust and gratitude. Grasping hands are a metaphor for lack of trust. With open hands, we recognize our need for God's grace. We recognize that it is only by God's grace that we are able to become the holy people he has called us to be. As we recognize our own need for and dependence on God's grace, we grow in humility. We come to see God as holy, loving, gracious, and powerful, and we come to see ourselves as recipients of God's mercy (1 Peter 1:3).

Most of our English translations urge us to "humble" ourselves, but in Greek the verb is passive. It encourages us to be humbled under the mighty hand of God. In other words, our capacity for humility also comes from God. We can think about the audience of 1 Peter and the suffering they endure. Their suffering has resulted in a humble position—resident aliens—in their culture. But their humble state is completely in God's control. He is the one who allows them to be humbled. And, he is the one who will lift them up. In the first-century world, where honor and shame were key values, being exalted is the honorable contrast to humility. Their honor is in God's hand. When the time is right in God's eyes, he will raise them up from their humble position. Meanwhile, they are to trust that their position, their status, is in God's hands.

No matter what position they are in, they are to cast their anxieties on God. Life in this world brings about events and experiences that can cause worry and anxiety. Our audience may be particularly worried about the need to defend their faith in public (3:15) or about the trials they face (1:6) or about their unbelieving family members (3:1). Whatever their worry or concern, they are to entrust it to God. They are instructed to cast *all* their anxieties on God. He can handle every one of them. There is no need to keep some back. The reason they are to do this is because of God's attitude toward them. God cares about them.

There are practical ways that Christians learn to cast their anxieties on the Lord. In prayer we name our anxiety before God and ask to grow in our capacity to trust God in everything. Some find it helpful to journal about their concerns and ask God to enter into the problems they described. Reading Scripture to be reminded of God's love and care for his children is another way to address anxiety. And meeting with wise Christian leaders who can help with specific worries can be helpful.

1. How have you been able to trust that your honor, status, or position are in God's hands?

2. How are you learning to cast your cares and anxieties on the Lord?

FOUR

Resist the Adversary

1 Peter 5:8–11 ESV *Be sober-minded; be watchful. Your adversary the devil prowls around like a roaring lion, seeking someone to devour. ⁹Resist him, firm in your faith, knowing that the same kinds of suffering are being experienced by your brotherhood throughout the world. ¹⁰And after you have suffered a little while, the God of all grace, who has called you to his eternal glory in Christ, will himself restore, confirm, strengthen, and establish you. ¹¹To him be the dominion forever and ever. Amen.*

Key Observation. Christians have a powerful adversary, the devil. But he can be resisted, and God's promises are trustworthy.

Understanding the Word. This is the third time that Peter has instructed his audience to be sober-minded. The first set of instructions that Peter gave starting in 1:13 was framed with the idea of being self-controlled. Then, in 4:7, Peter reminds them that the end of all things is at hand, and he commands them to be sober-minded. Now, at the very end of the letter, he repeats the instruction to be sober-minded. Peter wants those to whom he is speaking to be self-controlled (not out of control, like someone who is drunk). He wants them to be alert. He wants them to be watchful.

It is important to be completely clearheaded when there is an enemy on the prowl that is seeking to destroy the people of God. That opponent is the devil. The word "devil" has the underlying meaning of "someone who slanders." And this is the main form of suffering that the Christians are encountering. Throughout 1 Peter people speak evil of the Christians, mock them, and abuse them. Now we see that behind all of this is the enemy of God, the devil. One of the evils that the devil uses is false speech (lies, slander, slurs, insults). The devil's hope is to destroy faith and ultimately the new life that God is growing in his people. Peter compares the devil to a roaring lion that is seeking someone to devour. The lion roars when it is hungry and ready to begin the hunt for food. And Christians should know that this is a formidable enemy.

However, the devil can be resisted. The devil will cause suffering as a means of destroying Christians. But Peter's message is that suffering for one's faith is actually a sign of right relationship with God. Christians should not be discouraged if they suffer because of their faith. Instead, they should look forward to the future promise of God. Their experience of suffering is not unique. Other people throughout the world have also suffered because of their faith. But their suffering will not go on forever. After they have suffered for a little while God will restore them. No matter how long their suffering lasts—a few days or ending in martyrdom—they are reminded that God has called them and that God will share his glory with them. Through Christ they are enabled to enter into the amazing presence of God. He promises that he will set them in a secure place. They will be restored, secure, established, and built up. When God has done this for them, their adversary will no longer threaten them. Ultimately God is the one in control. He has been given power (dominion) over all things in every time and place. God's control extends into eternity. This is the one to whom they belong. This is the one in whom they can put their trust.

1. How do the instructions to be sober-minded and watchful relate to your experience of the world around you?

2. What promises of God give you hope and enable you to live out the Christian life today?

3. Do you believe that the devil is actively seeking to destroy Christians, and are you actively resisting the devil?

FIVE

Closing Remarks

1 Peter 5:12–14 ESV *By Silvanus, a faithful brother as I regard him, I have written briefly to you, exhorting and declaring that this is the true grace of God. Stand firm in it. [13]She who is at Babylon, who is likewise chosen, sends you greetings, and so does Mark, my son. [14]Greet one another with the kiss of love. Peace to all of you who are in Christ.*

Key Observation. Peter commends the letter carrier, encourages his listeners to steadfast faith, and sends greetings from the church.

Understanding the Word. First Peter ends with a typical letter closing. Peter introduces us to a few people who want to send their greetings. He restates his reasons for sending the letter. And he gives one final blessing to the churches in Asia Minor.

This letter is being sent to several churches that are spread out over a large area. In the first century, the best way to send a letter would be to have an emissary who would carry it from place to place. This person would read the letter out loud to the gathered community. They would also be able to help the audience interpret the letter's meaning. Silvanus is the letter carrier. Peter testifies that he is a "faithful brother." In other words, he is part of the family, the household, of God too. As such, he is to be treated as any brother in the family is to be treated—with love, hospitality, and humility.

Peter then says that his letter is brief and states the purpose behind his letter. He wrote to exhort the believers. This is another way to talk about encouragement. He knows that this group of Christians is experiencing suffering and exclusion. He is writing to encourage them in their faith and to give them hope in their suffering. He does this by declaring that the message in his letter is the true grace of God. From the beginning of the letter, Peter described the great gifts that they received from God: being chosen by God, being given new birth into a new family with an indestructible inheritance, and being allowed to suffer on account of God's name. In the midst of their suffering on behalf of the name of Jesus, they should remember their new family and especially the

Father who gave them new life. This will help them to be steady and secure, unwavering in their faith.

Peter sends greetings from the church in Rome. He uses the name "Babylon" as code for Rome. The city of Babylon known from Israel's exile was abandoned by the first century. Christians began to refer to Rome as "Babylon" as a way of describing a city that was powerful, wealthy, and opposed to God's people. Instead of critiquing the capital of the Roman Empire openly, this allowed them to make that critique in a subversive way. Even in the heart of the empire, there was a church—a group chosen by God just as they were. Mark also sends his greetings. Tradition has it that "Mark" refers to John Mark, who traveled with Paul (Acts 12–15) and who became a disciple of Peter's in Rome.

The letter ends with a final instruction and blessing. They are to greet one another with a loving kiss. To a group of people who are living in challenging times, Peter leaves them with the hope that they will experience the peace that flows from Christ.

1. As you think back over your study of 1 Peter, what is the most important thing you have learned or what has stood out to you the most?

2. Have you experienced Peter's letter as encouraging or as a letter about God's grace? If so, how?

WEEK EIGHT

GATHERING DISCUSSION OUTLINE

A. **Open session in prayer.** Ask that God would astonish us anew with fresh insight from God's Word and transform us into the disciples that Jesus desires us to become.

B. **Read:** 1 Peter 5:1–14. You might consider having each member of the group read a verse or asking several people to each read three or four verses.

C. **View video for this week's readings.**

D. What were key insights or takeaways that you gained from your reading during the week and from watching the video commentary? In particular, how did these help you to grow in your faith and understanding of Scripture this week? What parts of the Bible lesson or study raised questions for you?

E. **One main point from this week is:** *Are you living humbly? Are you watching out for the enemy, who wants you to fail? Remember: God cares for you and wants you to have peace.*

F. **Discuss questions selected from the daily readings.**

1. **KEY OBSERVATION:** Peter identifies himself as a leader and urges leaders in the church to care for God's flock.

   DISCUSSION QUESTION: Share some examples of leaders you have known whose lives present a model of godly living to their followers. Are you living in such a way that your life can be an example for others?

2. **KEY OBSERVATION:** The whole church is to practice humility toward one another.

    DISCUSSION QUESTION: In what ways can we practice humility in our own discipleship?

3. **KEY OBSERVATION:** Our lives are in God's control, and he cares for us.

    DISCUSSION QUESTION: How are you are learning to cast your cares and anxieties on the Lord?

4. **KEY OBSERVATION:** Christians have a powerful adversary, the devil. But he can be resisted, and God's promises are trustworthy

    DISCUSSION QUESTION: What promises of God give you hope and enable you to live out the Christian life today?

5. **KEY OBSERVATION:** Peter commends the letter carrier, encourages his listeners to steadfast faith, and sends greetings from the church.

    DISCUSSION QUESTION: As you think back over your study of 1 Peter, what is the most important thing you have learned or what has stood out to you the most?

G. **As the study concludes, consider specific ways that this week's Bible lesson invites you to grow and calls you to change.** How do this week's scriptures call us to think differently? How do they challenge us to change in order to align ourselves with God's work in the world? What specific actions should we take to apply the insights of the lesson to our daily lives? What kind of person does our Bible lesson call us to become?

H. **Close session with prayer.** Emphasize God's ongoing work of transformation in our lives in preparation for loving mission and service in the world.

SUGGESTED RESOURCES
FOR FURTHER READING

Davids, Peter. *A Theology of James, Peter, and Jude: Living in Light of the Coming King*. Grand Rapids: Zondervan, 2014.

Green, Joel B. *1 Peter*. Two Horizons Commentary Series. Grand Rapids: Eerdmans, 2007.

Jobes, Karen. *1 Peter*. Baker Exegetical Commentary on the New Testament. Grand Rapids: Baker, 2005.